MONSTER
GOOSE

MONSTER GOOSE

BY Judy Sierra

ILLUSTRATED BY Jack E. Davis

GULLIVER BOOKS   HARCOURT, INC.   SAN DIEGO   NEW YORK   LONDON

www.harcourt.com

Gulliver Books is a trademark of Harcourt, Inc., registered in the United States of America and/or other jurisdictions.

Library of Congress Cataloging-in-Publication Data
Sierra, Judy.
Monster Goose/written by Judy Sierra; illustrated by Jack E. Davis.
p.   cm.
"Gulliver Books."
Summary: A collection of twenty-five nursery rhymes, rewritten to feature vampires,
ghouls, mummies, the Loch Ness monster, and other fearsome creatures.
1. Monsters—Juvenile poetry.   2. Children's poetry, American.   3. Nursery rhymes—Adaptations.
[1. Nursery rhymes.   2. Monsters—Poetry.   3. American poetry.]
I. Davis, Jack E., ill.   II. Title.
PS3569.I39M66   2001
811'.54—dc21   00-8808
ISBN 0-15-202034-9

First edition

A C E G H F D B

PRINTED IN SINGAPORE

For my parents,
Jean Goose and Joe Gander
—J. S.

For Tommy and Bess
—J. E. D.

Old Monster Goose

Old Monster Goose,
When conditions did suit her,
Pecked out these rhymes
On her laptop computer.

Mary Had a Vampire Bat

Mary had a vampire bat.
His fur was black as night.
He followed her to school one day
And promised not to bite.
She brought him out for show-and-tell;
The teacher screamed and ran.
And school was canceled for a week,
Just as Mary planned.

Corpus McCool

Corpus McCool, the clumsy old ghoul,
Was interred near the gardens at Kew.
He lost his head in the cabbage bed,
And it later appeared in a stew.

Little Miss Mummy

Little Miss Mummy
Lay on her tummy
Smoking a big cigar.
A very large spider
Resided inside her.
(She kept all her guts in a jar.)

Humpty Dumpty

Humpty Dumpty swam in the sea.
Humpty's sunscreen was SPF-3.
Because he was so lightly oiled,
Dear Humpty ended up hard-boiled.

Pirate Pete

Pirate Pete and Pete's pet shark
Prowl the ocean after dark.
Sailing north and sailing south,
The shark up front with open mouth,
Guided by electric eels,
They search for unsuspecting meals.
So when you take a midnight dip,
Please keep an eye out for Pete's ship.

Rub-a-Dub-Dub

Rub-a-dub-dub,
Three fish in a tub.
And what do you think they do?
Because they're piranhas
With very poor manners,
They hide and wait for you.

Jill and Jacques

Jill and Jacques
Went to the loch
To fetch a pail of water.
Jill took a swim.
Events turned grim.
The famous monster caught her.

There Was an Old Zombie

There was an old zombie who lived
    in a shoe.
She had so many maggots, she didn't
    know what to do.
So she soaked them in soapsuds and
    painted them green.
She'll be giving them out next
    Halloween.

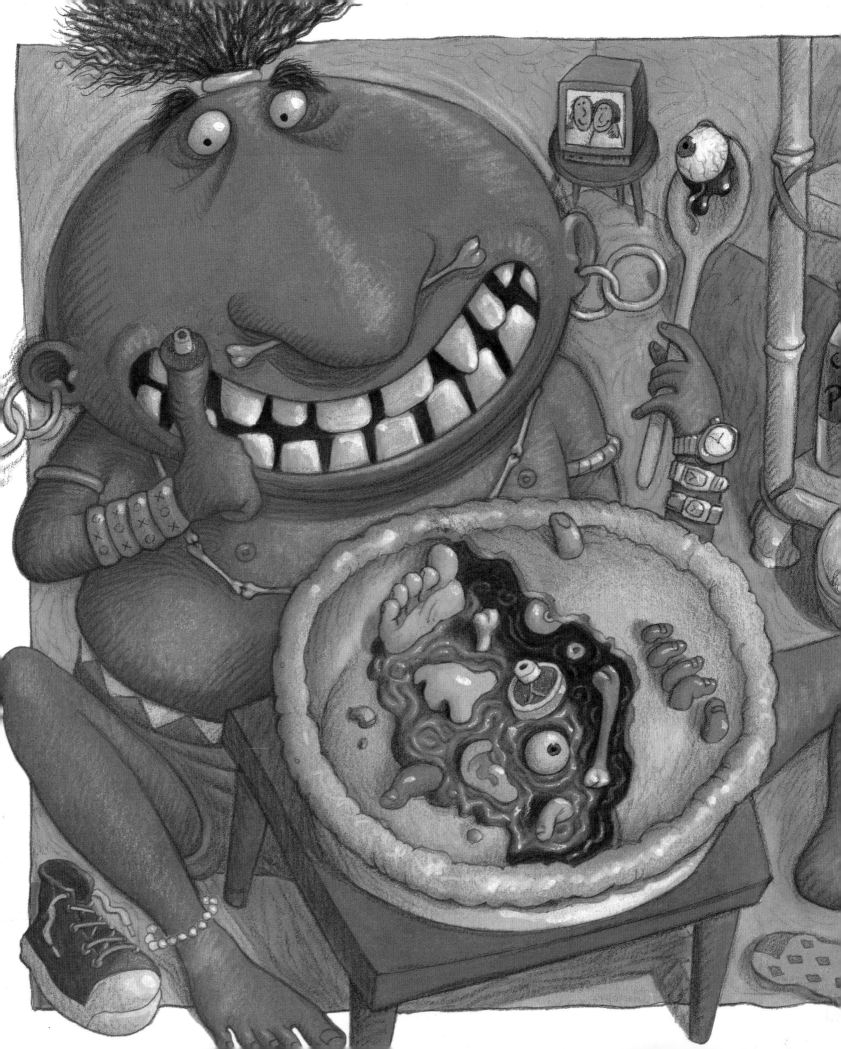

Cannibal Horner

Cannibal Horner
Sat in the corner
Eating a people potpie.
He bit his own thumb
And cried, "Oh, yum, yum,
A tasty young morsel am I!"

Pussycat, Pussycat

Pussycat, pussycat, where have you been?
—I've been to London to torment
 the queen.
Mean little pussycat, what did you there?
—I put a wee mouse in her long
 underwear.

Weird Mother Hubbard

Weird Mother Hubbard went down to
    the graveyard
To fetch her poor doggy a bone.
But that bone was the toe of Skeleton Joe.
When she took it, Joe followed her home.

She went to the tailor's
To buy Joe a coat,
But when she came back
He was shaving the goat.

She went to the hatter's
To buy Joe a hat,
But when she came back
He was painting the cat.

She went to the baker's
To buy Joe some bread,
But when she came back
He was juggling his head.

The dog said politely,
"This guest has to go."
So Weird Mother Hubbard said,
"TAKE BACK YOUR TOE!"

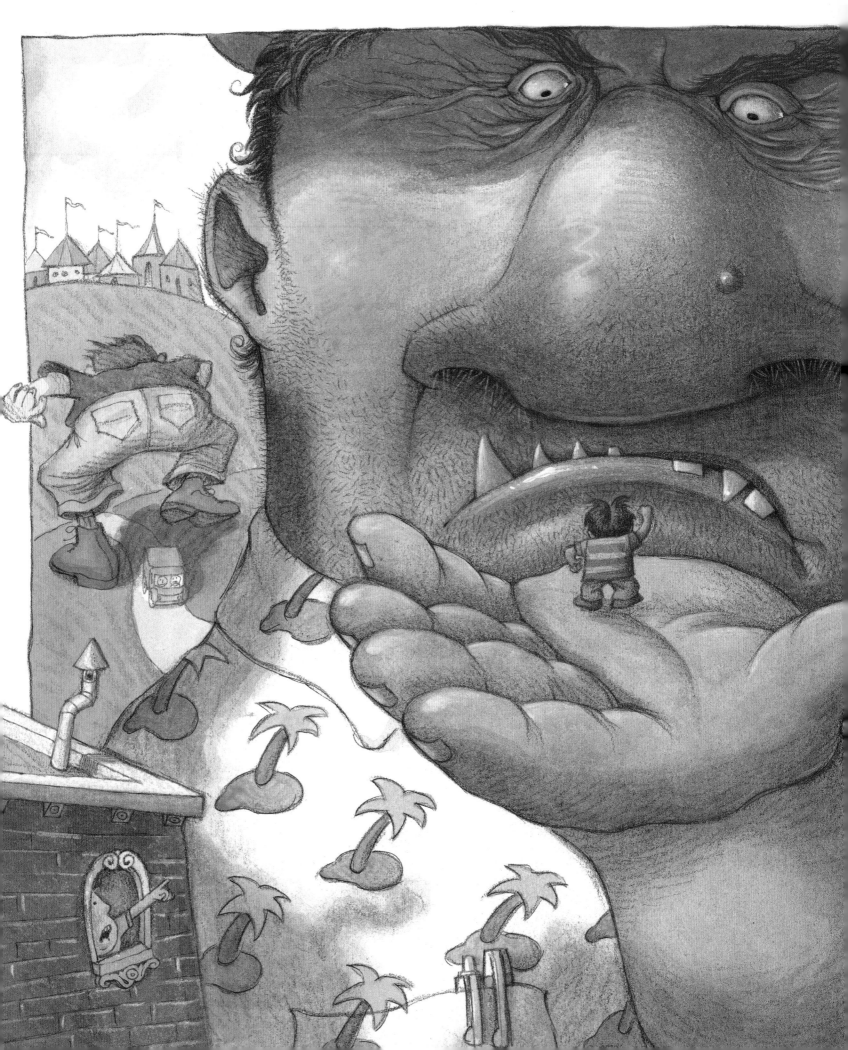

Billy Bryant

Billy Bryant met a giant
Going to the fair.
The giant growled at Billy Bryant,
"Would you like a scare?"
Said Billy Bryant to the giant,
"That would not be fair.
The last three giants that *I* scared
Are in intensive care."

Jack Sprat

Jack Sprat
Ate some fat
And drank some gasoline.
He lit his pipe
And in one swipe
Invented Lean Cuisine.

Hush, Little Monster

Hush, little monster, don't you whine,
Papa's gonna give you to Frankenstein.
If you and Frank can't get along,
Papa's gonna send you to old King Kong.
If you don't like that big gorilla,
You might prefer his friend Godzilla.
If giant lizards make you scared,
Maybe you'll be happy with a grizzly bear.
If life in a bear cave isn't fun,
Why not visit an alien?
If flying through space upsets
      your tummy,
Just come on home to your pappy
      and your mummy.

Slithery, Dithery, Dock

Slithery, dithery, dock,
The snake slid up the clock.
She soon grew bored
And bit the cord.
It gave her quite a shock.
The snake began to quake.
The clock began to rock.
At half past four
They struck the floor.
Smashery, squashery, dock!

There Is a Hungry Boggart

There is a hungry boggart
Living somewhere near my bed.
He gobbled up the sheets
And munched the pillow 'neath my head.
He nibbled my pajamas,
And he swallowed all my toys.
I'm really quite relieved
He has an allergy to boys.

Young King Cole

Young King Cole was a terrible troll:
He washed his feet in the toilet bowl,
Brushed his teeth with turpentine,
And combed his hair with a porcupine.

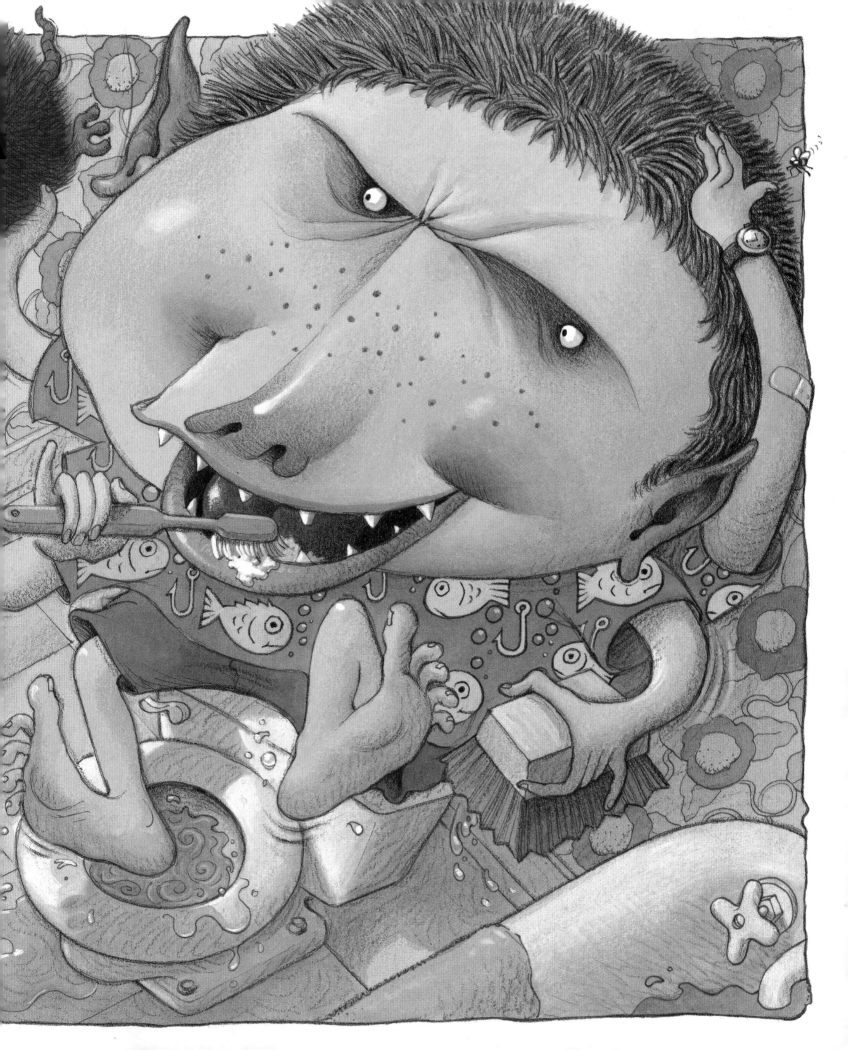

Mistress Mary

Mistress Mary. Scary? Very!
Her garden is not ordinary:
Her green beans are mean,
    and her chives carry knives.
Her catnip just caught a canary.
A killer potato ate all her tomatoes,
And now he is looking for Mary.

Sing a Song of Sea Slime

Sing a song of sea slime, sewer gas,
  and sludge.
Four and twenty wharf rats dipped in
  mocha fudge.
When the dish was served, it scampered
  out the door.
"Dessert has fled," the poor king said.
  "I guess I'll lick the floor."

The Itsy-Bitsy Spider

The itsy-bitsy spider
Climbed up the warthog's snout.
The warthog grabbed a hankie
And tried to blow it out.
The little bloke was blasted
All the way to Spain,
So the itsy-bitsy spider
Did not go there again.

Since different dye lots of a color may vary, purchase enough yarn at one time to finish your item. To estimate the amount of yarn needed, either refer to a similar project or work a skein in the desired pattern and gauge, measure the result, and divide it into the total size.

The wrapper around each skein or ball of yarn states yarn type, skein weight, fiber content, color, and dye lot number; sometimes included is whether yarn is mothproof, colorfast, preshrunk or machine washable. However, it is always wise to test colorfastness and shrink resistance by crocheting a 6″ square swatch and washing it before beginning your project.

Ball winding. Most yarns are packaged in ready-to-use balls or pull skeins; others, in "butterfly" skeins that must be wound in a ball. Wind loosely to avoid stretching the yarn. Loop the skein around a chair back, a helper's hands, or a yarn winder (facing page), cut the tie that holds the skein together, and start the ball by winding the yarn over the fingers of one hand. After a number of turns, remove the yarn, turn it parallel to the fingers, and resume winding around the fingers (and the wound yarn). Continue in this fashion, changing direction occasionally.

Crochet hooks come in steel, aluminum, plastic, and wood and are sized according to thickness. The finer the yarn, the smaller the size hook used; the thicker the yarn, the larger the size hook used. *Steel hooks,* the finest, are used mainly with fingering yarn, thin linen, and cotton. They are numbered in reverse order from 14 (smallest) to 00 (largest). *Aluminum and plastic hooks,* used mainly with wool and synthetic yarns and coarse cotton, are sized in increasing order from B (smallest) to K, then jump to Q (largest). The B hook is about equal to an 00 steel hook. Some manufacturers size these hooks by number. *Wooden hooks,* used mainly with heavy, bulky yarn, come 10 (smallest), 13, 14, and 15 (largest). *Afghan hooks,* used for the Afghan stitch, look like knitting needles with a crochet hook at one end. They are aluminum, come in two lengths, 10″ and 14″, and are sized in increasing order by letter, B–K, and by number 1–10½.

YARNS

1. Knitting worsted (wool)
2. Knitting worsted (orlon)
3. 10/2 linen
4. Rug yarn (wool)
5. Rug yarn (75% rayon, 25% cotton)
6. Rug yarn (100% acrylic)
7. Sport yarn
8. Knit-Cro-Sheen/Pearl cotton/Carpet warp

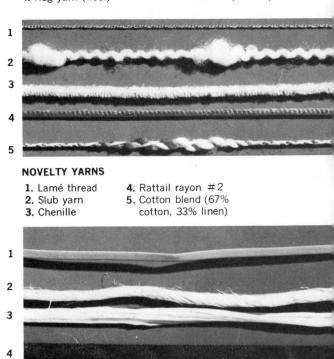

NOVELTY YARNS

1. Lamé thread
2. Slub yarn
3. Chenille
4. Rattail rayon #2
5. Cotton blend (67% cotton, 33% linen)

OTHER MATERIALS
1. Plastic lanyard
2. Sisal twine
3. Raffia
4. Ribbon
5. Celtagil (straw)

CROCHET HOOK SIZES—ALUMINUM OR PLASTIC

American	K/10½	J/10	I/9	H/8	G/6	F/5	E/4	D/3	C/2	B/1
English	2	4	5	6	7	8	9	10	11	12
Continental mm. (metric)	7	6	5.5	5	4.5	4	3.5		3	2.5

Slip knot

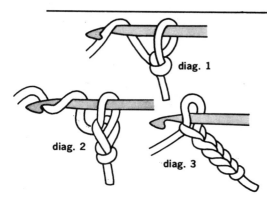

Holding the work. Note that hook is held in the same manner as a table-knife in cutting position.

STARTING THE WORK RIGHT-HANDED

All crochet begins with a slip knot. Make a loop about 4″ from yarn end and hold between thumb and forefinger. Place yarn strand behind loop and draw through as shown. Pull yarn ends to tighten loop, but not so tight that hook cannot pass through freely.

Holding the work. You may find holding the work awkward at first, but ease will come with practice. The principle is to arrange the yarn so that it feeds easily and at a regulated tension, and to hold the hook in a comfortable position. One way to arrange yarn is to loop it around forefinger and hold it in place under last two fingers and against palm. Hold base of stitch between thumb and middle finger. Photo shows how to hold hook: as you would a knife in a cutting position—between thumb and forefinger and resting lightly on the other fingers. (Hook can also be held as you would a pencil, bringing middle finger forward to rest near tip.)

ABBREVIATED CROCHET TERMS

beg—beginning	**rep(s)**—repeat(s).
ch(s)—chain(s) or chain stitch	**rnd**—round
cl—cluster	**sc**—single crochet
dc—double crochet	**sk**—skip
dec(s)—decrease(s)	**sl st**—slip stitch
dtr—double triple crochet	**sp(s)**—space(s)
hdc—half double crochet	**st(s)**—stitch(es)
inc(s)—increase(s)	**tog**—together
lp(s)—loop(s)	**tr**—triple crochet
pat—pattern	**tr tr**—triple triple crochet
pr r—previous row or round	**yo**—yarn over hook

---

*—repeat instructions from asterisk as many more times as directed in addition to the original

x—times

( )—work instructions in parentheses as many times as directed, for example: (2 sc into next dc) 3x means to work stitches enclosed in parentheses 3 times in all

---

diag. 1

diag. 2

diag. 3

CHAIN STITCH (ch)

All crochet builds on a base of chain stitches.

1. Pass hook under yarn and catch yarn with hook **(diag. 1)**. This is called yarn over hook (yo).

2. Draw yarn through loop on hook **(diag. 2)**. Do not work tightly. One chain stitch (ch) completed.

3. Continue to yarn over and draw through a new loop **(diag. 3)** for the number of chain stitches required. Keep thumb and forefinger near stitch (st) you are working on. This keeps chain from twisting.

Unless directions specify otherwise: *Always* insert hook under the *two top* loops (strands) of a stitch. *Always* insert hook from *front* to *back*. There will *always* be one loop left on hook. *Do not work tightly.*

Practice each stitch until you are familiar with it. Start your practice piece on a chain of 15 to 20 stitches, using knitting worsted and an I or J hook.

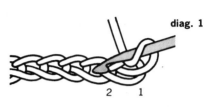

diag. 1

SINGLE CROCHET STITCH (sc)

Single crochet is the shortest of the basic stitches.

Make a chain of desired length.

1. Insert hook under the two top loops in 2nd chain stitch (ch) from hook **(diag. 1).**

2. Yarn over hook **(diag. 2A)** and draw yarn through chain stitch. There are now 2 loops on hook **(diag. 2B).**

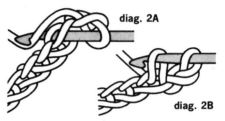

diag. 2A

diag. 2B

3. Yarn over hook **(diag. 3A)** and draw it through the 2 loops on hook **(diag. 3B).** This completes one single crochet (sc).

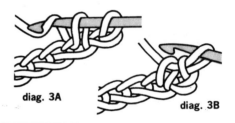

diag. 3A

diag. 3B

4. Insert hook into next chain stitch **(diag. 4).** Repeat steps 2 and 3 and work a single crochet in each chain across.

diag. 4

5. At end of row, chain 1 **(diag. 5)** and turn work so reverse side is facing you.

diag. 5

6. On following rows, insert hook in first stitch (st) of previous row **(diags. 6A, 6B).** Repeat steps 2 and 3 and do single crochet in each st across. Chain (ch) 1 and turn.

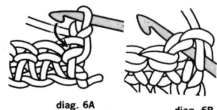

diag. 6A

diag. 6B

diag. 1

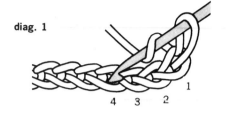

DOUBLE CROCHET STITCH (dc)

Double crochet is twice as tall as single crochet. These two stitches are the ones most commonly used.

Make a chain of desired length.

1. Yarn over hook (yo) and insert hook into 4th chain stitch (ch) from hook **(diag. 1).**

---

diag. 2

2. Yo and draw yarn through **(diag. 2).** There are now 3 loops on hook.

---

diag. 3A

diag. 3B

3. Yo **(diag. 3A),** and draw yarn through 2 loops. There are now 2 loops on hook **(diag. 3B).**

---

diag. 4A

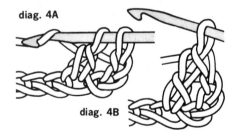

diag. 4B

4. Yo and draw yarn through the 2 loops (lps) on hook **(diag. 4A).** One double crochet (dc) completed **(diag. 4B).**

---

diag. 5A

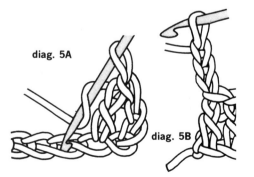

diag. 5B

5. Yo and insert hook into next ch **(diag. 5A).** Repeat (rep) steps 2–4 and make a dc in each ch across. At end of row, ch 3 **(diag. 5B)** and turn.

6. On following rows, skip first st, yo, and insert hook into 2nd st **(diag. 6)**. (The turning ch-3 at end of previous row counts as first dc of next row; therefore first dc of every row is always skipped.) Rep steps 2–4 and do dc in each st across.

diag. 6

7. Work last dc of row in 3rd ch of turning ch-3 of previous row **(diag. 7)**. This keeps the work even. Ch 3 and turn.

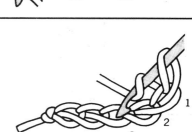

diag. 7

HALF DOUBLE CROCHET STITCH (hdc)

Taller than single crochet but not so tall as double crochet.

Make a chain of desired length.

1. Yo and insert hook into 3rd ch from hook **(diag. 1)**.

diag. 1

2. Yo and draw yarn through ch. There are now 3 loops (lps) on hook **(diag. 2A)**. Yo and draw through the 3 lps on hook **(diag. 2B)**. One half double crochet (hdc) completed.

diag. 2A

3. Yo, insert hook into next ch. Rep step 2 and do hdc in each ch across. At end of row ch 2 and turn.

4. On following rows, yo and insert hook in first st (in hdc, the turning ch does not count as first hdc). Rep step 2 and do hdc in each st across. Ch 2 and turn.

diag. 2B

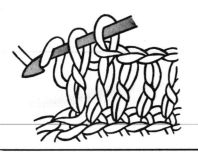

INCREASE (inc)

An increase is usually made by working two sts in the same st, but it may also be made, in any st but sc, by working a st in the very first st—the one usually skipped because of the turning chain.

DECREASE (dec)

To decrease in single crochet: Insert hook into st, yo and draw through a lp. Insert hook into next st, yo and draw through a lp. Yo and draw through the 3 lps on hook.

To decrease in double crochet: (yo, insert hook into next st and draw through a lp, yo and draw through 2 lps)2x. (3 lps on hook) Yo and draw through the remaining 3 lps.

To dec in other sts, just inc the number of lps on hook. A dec can also be made by skipping first st at beginning of row. Dec at end of row by skipping next to last st.

TRIPLE CROCHET STITCH (tr)

Taller than double crochet, it produces looser work. *Note:* The popular name of this stitch and its variations is treble crochet, but the term triple crochet is used here since it fits better with single and double crochet.

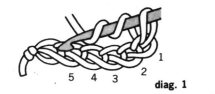

5 4 3 2 1 **diag. 1**

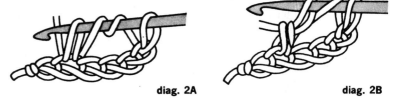

diag. 2A   **diag. 2B**

diag. 3

Make a chain of desired length.

1. Yo twice and insert hook into 5th ch from hook **(diag. 1)**.

2. Yo, draw through a lp (4 lps on hook; **diag. 2A),** yo, draw through 2 lps on hook (3 lps on hook, **diag. 2B)**. Yo and draw through 2 lps on hook 2 more times. One tr completed.

3. Yo twice and insert hook into next ch **(diag. 3)**. Rep step 2. Do a tr in each ch across. At end of row, ch 4, turn.

4. On following rows, insert hook into 2nd st (turning ch counts as first tr of next row). Work last tr of row in 4th ch of turning ch of previous row **(diag. 7,** page 15). Ch 4, turn.

DOUBLE TRIPLE CROCHET STITCH (dtr)

One stitch taller than triple crochet, it is worked with an extra step, as follows: Yo 3 times, insert hook into 6th ch from hook, yo, draw through lp (5 lps on hook), yo, draw through 2 lps at a time, 4 times. One dtr completed **(diag. A)**. Ch 5 to turn. Insert hook into 2nd st of next row.

TRIPLE TRIPLE CROCHET (tr tr)

The tallest of the sts, it produces the loosest work. Yo 4 times, insert hook into 7th ch and continue by working an extra step throughout **(diag. B)**. Ch 6 to turn. Insert hook into 2nd st of next row.

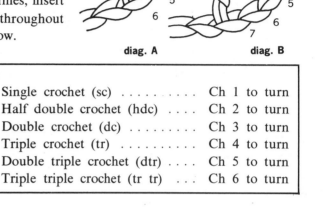

diag. A   diag. B

TO TURN WORK

Each stitch uses a different number of chain stitches to turn at the end of a row so as to bring the work into position for the next row. The length of the turning ch depends upon the length of the stitch that will be used to begin the row. Listed right for easy reference are the turning chs for the basic sts.

Single crochet (sc)	Ch 1 to turn
Half double crochet (hdc)	Ch 2 to turn
Double crochet (dc)	Ch 3 to turn
Triple crochet (tr)	Ch 4 to turn
Double triple crochet (dtr)	Ch 5 to turn
Triple triple crochet (tr tr) . . .	Ch 6 to turn

SLIP STITCH (sl st)

A joining stitch used to form a chain into a ring, to join a round, or to join pieces invisibly. Also used to work across stitches for shaping or to strengthen edges. It adds no height to the work. When crochet directions say join, always do so with a sl st. A sl st is worked by inserting hook into a st, yo (diag.) and drawing yarn through st and lp on hook in one motion.

To form a ring: Make a chain. Insert hook in first ch **(diag. A)**, yo, and pull through ch and loop on hook in one motion **(diag. B)**.

To make a round (rnd): Make a ring. For the first round (each time around is called a "round") work the stated number of stitches into ring **(diag. C)**. Work next round into stitches of first round. Continue in this fashion, working each rnd into sts of previous rnd.

diag. A

diag. B

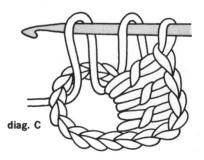

diag. C

diag. 1A

diag. 1B

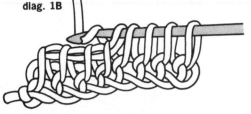

diag. 2A

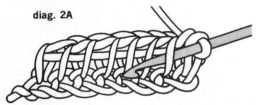

diag. 2B

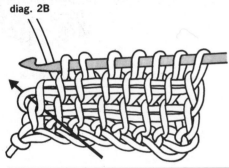

AFGHAN STITCH

This stitch is completed in two rows (referred to as one row in instructions). In the first half, leave all loops on hook; in the second half, work loops off. *Do not turn work throughout.* Use an afghan hook.

Make a chain of desired length. *Note: On ch row only,* insert hook through *one* top loop instead of two.

Row 1:

A. Insert hook into top lp of 2nd ch from hook, yo, draw through a lp. Rep in each ch across **(diag. 1A)**. *Leave all loops on hook.*

B. Work off loops. Yo, draw through first lp on hook, * yo and draw through 2 lps, rep from * across **(diag. 1B)**. The loop remaining on hook counts as first st of next row.

Row 2:

A. Keeping all lps on hook, insert hook under 2nd vertical bar **(diag. 2A)**, yo, and draw through a lp. Rep for each bar across, ending insert hook under last bar and the st directly behind it, yo and draw through a lp **(diag. 2B)**. This makes a firm edge.

B. Rep row 1B.

Rep row 2 for pattern. To finish, sl st in each bar across.

DECREASE FOR AFGHAN STITCH

To dec one st, insert hook under the next 2 vertical bars, yo, and draw through a loop (diag.).

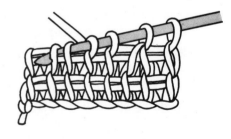

INCREASE FOR AFGHAN STITCH

To inc one st, insert hook into ch between the next 2 vertical bars, yo, and pull through a loop (diag.). Insert hook under next vertical bar, yo and pull through a loop.

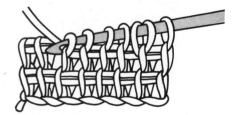

STARTING THE WORK LEFT-HANDED

All crochet begins with a slip knot. Make a loop about 4″ from yarn end and hold between thumb and forefinger. Place yarn strand behind loop and draw through as shown. Pull yarn ends to tighten loop, but not so tight that hook cannot pass through freely.

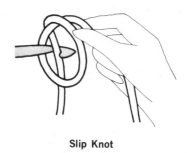

Slip Knot

Holding the work. You may find holding the work awkward at first, but ease will come with practice. The principle is to arrange the yarn so that it feeds easily and at a regulated tension, and to hold the hook in a comfortable position. One way to arrange yarn is to loop it around forefinger and hold it in place under last two fingers and against palm. Hold base of stitch between thumb and middle finger. Photo shows how to hold hook: as you would a knife in a cutting position—between thumb and forefinger and resting lightly on the other fingers. (Hook can also be held as you would a pencil, bringing middle finger forward to rest near tip.)

Holding the work. Note that hook is held in the same manner as a table-knife in cutting position.

ABBREVIATED CROCHET TERMS

beg—beginning	**rep(s)**—repeat(s)
ch(s)—chain(s) or chain stitch	**rnd**—round
cl—cluster	**sc**—single crochet
dc—double crochet	**sk**—skip
dec(s)—decrease(s)	**sl st**—slip stitch
dtr—double triple crochet	**sp(s)**—space(s)
hdc—half double crochet	**st(s)**—stitch(es)
inc(s)—increase(s)	**tog**—together
lp(s)—loop(s)	**tr**—triple crochet
pat—pattern	**tr tr**—triple triple crochet
pr r—previous row or round	**yo**—yarn over hook

*—repeat instructions from asterisk as many more times as directed in addition to the original

x—times

( )—work instructions in parentheses as many times as directed, for example: (2 sc into next dc) 3x means to work stitches enclosed in parentheses 3 times in all

CHAIN STITCH (ch)

All crochet builds on a base of chain stitches.

1. Pass hook under yarn and catch yarn with hook **(diag. 1)**. This is called yarn over hook (yo).

2. Draw yarn through loop on hook **(diag. 2)**. Do not work tightly. One chain stitch (ch) completed.

3. Continue to yarn over and draw through a new loop **(diag. 3)** for the number of chain stitches required. Keep thumb and forefinger near stitch (st) you are working on. This keeps chain from twisting.

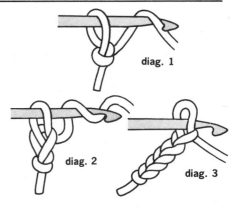

diag. 1

diag. 2

diag. 3

Unless directions specify otherwise: *Always* insert hook under the *two top* loops (strands) of a stitch. *Always* insert hook from *front* to *back*. There will *always* be one loop left on hook. *Do not work tightly.*

Practice each stitch until you are familiar with it. Start your practice piece on a chain of 15 to 20 stitches, using knitting worsted and an I or J hook.

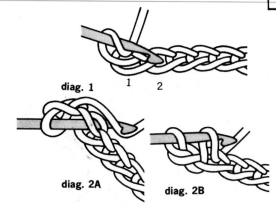

diag. 1

diag. 2A   diag. 2B

SINGLE CROCHET STITCH (sc)

Single crochet is the shortest of the basic stitches.

Make a chain of desired length.

1. Insert hook under the two top loops in 2nd chain stitch (ch) from hook **(diag. 1)**.

2. Yarn over hook **(diag. 2A)** and draw yarn through chain stitch. There are now 2 loops on hook **(diag. 2B).**

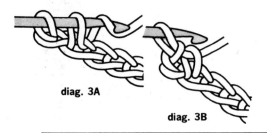

diag. 3A

diag. 3B

3. Yarn over hook **(diag. 3A)** and draw it through the 2 loops on hook **(diag. 3B).** This completes one single crochet (sc).

diag. 4

4. Insert hook into next chain stitch **(diag. 4).** Repeat steps 2 and 3 and work a single crochet in each chain across.

diag. 5

5. At end of row, chain 1 **(diag. 5)** and turn work so reverse side is facing you.

diag. 6A   diag. 6B

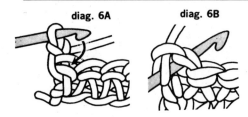

6. On following rows, insert hook in first stitch (st) of previous row **(diags. 6A, 6B).** Repeat steps 2 and 3 and do single crochet in each st across. Chain (ch) 1 and turn.

DOUBLE CROCHET STITCH (dc)

Double crochet is twice as tall as single crochet. These two stitches are the ones most commonly used.

Make a chain of desired length.

1. Yarn over hook (yo) and insert hook into 4th chain stitch (ch) from hook **(diag. 1).**

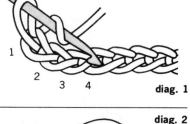

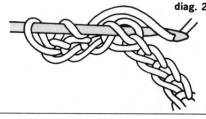

diag. 1

diag. 2

2. Yo and draw yarn through **(diag. 2).** There are now 3 loops on hook.

diag. 3A

3. Yo **(diag. 3A),** and draw yarn through 2 loops. There are now 2 loops on hook **(diag. 3B).**

diag. 3B

diag. 4B

4. Yo and draw yarn through the 2 loops (lps) on hook **(diag. 4A).** One double crochet (dc) completed **(diag. 4B).**

diag. 4A

5. Yo and insert hook into next ch **(diag. 5A).** Repeat (rep) steps 2–4 and make a dc in each ch across. At end of row, ch 3 **(diag. 5B)** and turn.

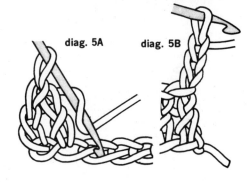

diag. 5A   diag. 5B

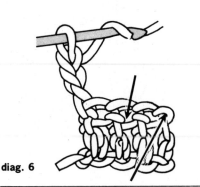

diag. 6

6. On following rows, skip first st, yo, and insert hook into 2nd st **(diag. 6).** (The turning ch-3 at end of previous row counts as first dc of next row; therefore first dc of every row is always skipped.) Rep steps 2–4 and do dc in each st across.

diag. 7

7. Work last dc of row in 3rd ch of turning ch-3 of previous row **(diag. 7).** This keeps the work even. Ch 3 and turn.

HALF DOUBLE CROCHET STITCH (hdc)
Taller than single crochet but not so tall as double crochet.

Make a chain of desired length.

1. Yo and insert hook into 3rd ch from hook **(diag. 1).**

diag. 1

2. Yo and draw yarn through ch. There are now 3 loops (lps) on hook **(diag. 2A).** Yo and draw through the 3 lps on hook **(diag. 2B).** One half double crochet (hdc) completed.

diag. 2A

3. Yo, insert hook into next ch. Rep step 2 and do hdc in each ch across. At end of row ch 2 and turn.

4. On following rows, yo and insert hook in first st (in hdc, the turning ch does not count as first hdc). Rep step 2 and do hdc in each st across. Ch 2 and turn.

diag. 2B

INCREASE (inc)

An increase is usually made by working two sts in the same st, but it may also be made, in any st but sc, by working a st in the very first st—the one usually skipped because of the turning chain.

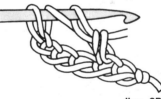

DECREASE (dec)

To decrease in single crochet: Insert hook into st, yo and draw through a lp. Insert hook into next st, yo and draw through a lp. Yo and draw through the 3 lps on hook.

To decrease in double crochet: (yo, insert hook into next st and draw through a lp, yo and draw through 2 lps)2x. (3 lps on hook) Yo and draw through the remaining 3 lps.

To dec in other sts, just inc the number of lps on hook. A dec can also be made by skipping first st at beginning of row. Dec at end of row by skipping next to last st.

TRIPLE CROCHET STITCH (tr)

Taller than double crochet, it produces looser work. *Note:* The popular name of this stitch and its variations is treble crochet, but the term triple crochet is used here since it fits better with single and double crochet.

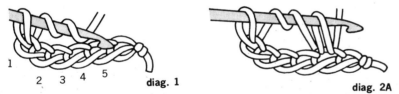

diag. 1

diag. 2A

diag. 2B

Make a chain of desired length.

1. Yo twice and insert hook into 5th ch from hook **(diag. 1).**

2. Yo, draw through a lp (4 lps on hook; **diag. 2A),** yo, draw through 2 lps on hook (3 lps on hook, **diag. 2B).** Yo and draw through 2 lps on hook 2 more times. One tr completed.

3. Yo twice and insert hook into next ch **(diag. 3).** Rep step 2. Do a tr in each ch across. At end of row, ch 4, turn.

4. On following rows, insert hook into 2nd st (turning ch counts as first tr of next row). Work last tr of row in 4th ch of turning ch of previous row **(diag. 7,** page 15). Ch 4, turn.

diag. 3

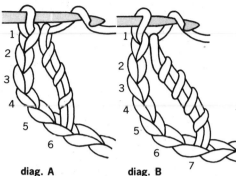

diag. A   diag. B

DOUBLE TRIPLE CROCHET STITCH (dtr)

One stitch taller than triple crochet, it is worked with an extra step, as follows: Yo 3 times, insert hook into 6th ch from hook, yo, draw through lp (5 lps on hook), yo, draw through 2 lps at a time, 4 times. One dtr completed **(diag. A)**. Ch 5 to turn. Insert hook into 2nd st of next row.

TRIPLE TRIPLE CROCHET (tr tr)

The tallest of the sts, it produces the loosest work. Yo 4 times, insert hook into 7th ch and continue by working an extra step throughout **(diag. B)**. Ch 6 to turn. Insert hook into 2nd st of next row.

TO TURN WORK

Each stitch uses a different number of chain stitches to turn at the end of a row so as to bring the work into position for the next row. The length of the turning ch depends upon the length of the stitch that will be used to begin the row. Listed right for easy reference are the turning chs for the basic sts.

Single crochet (sc)	Ch 1 to turn
Half double crochet (hdc)	Ch 2 to turn
Double crochet (dc)	Ch 3 to turn
Triple crochet (tr)	Ch 4 to turn
Double triple crochet (dtr)	Ch 5 to turn
Triple triple crochet (tr tr) . . .	Ch 6 to turn

SLIP STITCH (sl st)

A joining stitch used to form a chain into a ring, to join a round, or to join pieces invisibly. Also used to work across stitches for shaping or to strengthen edges. It adds no height to the work. When crochet directions say join, always do so with a sl st. A sl st is worked by inserting hook into a st, yo (diag.) and drawing yarn through st and lp on hook in one motion.

To form a ring: Make a chain. Insert hook in first ch **(diag. A)**, yo, and pull through ch and loop on hook in one motion **(diag. B)**.

To make a round (rnd): Make a ring. For the first round (each time around is called a "round") work the stated number of stitches into ring **(diag. C)**. Work next round into stitches of first round. Continue in this fashion, working each rnd into sts of previous rnd.

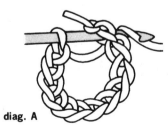

diag. A

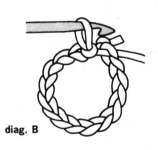

diag. B

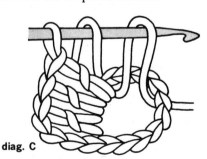

diag. C

AFGHAN STITCH

This stitch is completed in two rows (referred to as one row in instructions). In the first half, leave all loops on hook; in the second half, work loops off. *Do not turn work throughout.* Use an afghan hook.

Make a chain of desired length. *Note: On ch row only,* insert hook through *one* top loop instead of two.

Row 1:

A. Insert hook into top lp of 2nd ch from hook, yo, draw through a lp. Rep in each ch across **(diag. 1A).** *Leave all loops on hook.*

B. Work off loops. Yo, draw through first lp on hook, * yo and draw through 2 lps, rep from * across **(diag. 1B).** The loop remaining on hook counts as first st of next row.

Row 2:

A. Keeping all lps on hook, insert hook under 2nd vertical bar **(diag. 2A),** yo, and draw through a lp. Rep for each bar across, ending insert hook under last bar and the st directly behind it, yo and draw through a lp **(diag. 2B).** This makes a firm edge.

B. Rep row 1B.

Rep row 2 for pattern. To finish, sl st in each bar across.

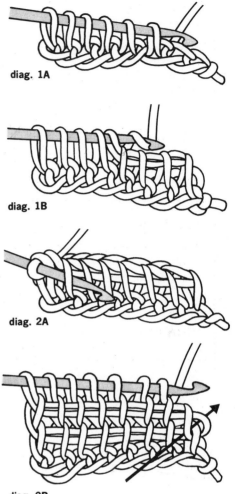

diag. 1A

diag. 1B

diag. 2A

diag. 2B

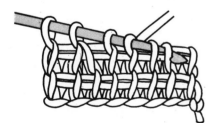

DECREASE FOR AFGHAN STITCH

To dec one st, insert hook under the next 2 vertical bars, yo, and draw through a loop (diag.).

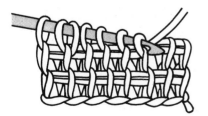

INCREASE FOR AFGHAN STITCH

To inc one st, insert hook into ch between the next 2 vertical bars, yo, and pull through a loop (diag.). Insert hook under next vertical bar, yo and pull through a loop.

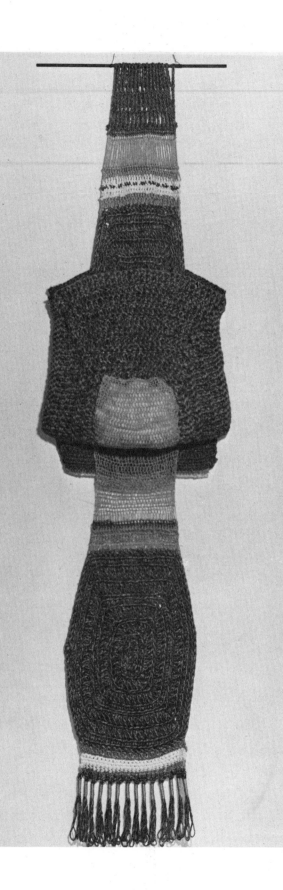

GAUGE

The gauge is the number of stitches and rows per inch. It determines the size of the item to be made and is always included in the directions. To check gauge, crochet and block a 4″ sq. swatch, using stitch, yarn, and hook specified. Place ruler on a row and count the number of stitches per inch; place ruler lengthwise and count the number of rows per inch. If the measure is greater than the gauge, change to a larger hook—you are working too tightly; if it is less, change to a smaller hook—you are working too loosely. Hook size does not matter so long as gauge is correct.

MULTIPLES

Multiple of chain refers to the amount of chain stitches that must be made at the start of a piece if the pattern is to work out correctly. For example, if instructions call for a multiple of 10 ch, then chain 20, 30, 40, or any amount evenly divisible by 10. If multiple is 10 + 2 ch, add 2 ch after the multiple is completed, for example, 22, 32, 42, etc.

Multiple of stitches refers to the number of sts in one pattern repeat. Should you wish to change to a different pattern in the course of your work, you would need to know its mult of sts. On page 80 is a list of multiples for pattern stitches and projects in this book.

BLOCKING

Blocking is used to shape a finished piece. Place piece on padded surface and pin sides, with heavy rustproof pins, while gently stretching to correct measurements. Place pins as close as necessary to obtain straight edges. Cover piece with a damp cloth and steam with an iron by supporting iron's weight in your hand and moving it above the piece *without touching it.* Remove pins when piece is thoroughly dry. If project is in sections, block each separately. Block raised or bulky patterns face up. Certain yarns do not require blocking, such as those sturdy enough to hold their shapes.

ENDING THE WORK

To fasten off, cut yarn leaving a 3″–4″ tail and pull it through final loop. Weave in all tails at end of work. **To weave in,** thread each tail end with a tapestry needle and weave through areas of solid crochet to fasten securely. Trim remainder close to work.

"Circes Mandrake" by Tony Tudin, approx. 20″ x 65″. Wall hanging worked in single and double crochet with dyed hemp, linen, wool, and string. 1970. Courtesy of The Canadian Guild of Crafts (Ontario) Canada.

JOINING

Sections are joined by slip stitching, sewing, or weaving them together. Use whatever method gives the best results. Join as invisibly as possible with matching yarn (unless seam is part of design). Do not pull tightly—seams should have elasticity.

Slip stitching. Pin pieces, wrong sides facing. Insert hook into top loops of both pieces, catch yarn, pull through, and knot over loops. Insert hook into same place, yo, and draw through. Insert into next loops, yo, and draw through loops on hook for first sl st. Continue along edges. Leave a 4″ tail to be woven in.

Sewing. Pin pieces right sides facing. Insert threaded tapestry needle through top loops of both pieces, leaving a 4″ tail. Secure stitch—do not knot. Sew close to edges.

Weaving. Lay pieces face up, edges meeting and follow diagram. Insert threaded tapestry needle in *center* of loops throughout. If edges are uneven, sew rather than weave.

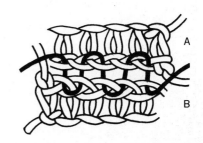

Weaving: pull up needle in A, insert from *wrong* side in B, * insert from *right* side in next B loop, insert from wrong side in next A loop, insert from right side in next A loop, insert from wrong side in next B loop. Repeat from *.

CHANGING COLOR

When directions say to change color, make stitch immediately preceding color change *by working last yo with 2nd color.* Leave tail. When changing for a few stitches or over small areas, twist 1st color around 2nd and carry it loosely across back until picked up again. Or "work over" it. This means laying 1st color across top of row being worked and working 2nd color over it until needed. This method makes for fewer ends to weave in at the finish. It may also result in an uneven stitch; to compensate, work tighter. However, if the 1st color is to be eliminated entirely, cut yarn *(break off)* and fasten. Or lay it on top of previous row, work over it for a few stitches, then break off. When working with more than four colors, you may want to use bobbins to keep yarn from tangling. Fill bobbins with color changes and refill as needed.

ATTACHING NEW STRAND

Insert hook into stitch, loop new strand over hook and pull through Remove hook, pull tail through and knot it to main strand. Insert hook into same place, catch yarn, pull through, and continue work.

ATTACHING NEW SKEIN

Attach new skein, preferably at the end of a row, leaving tails on both new and old skeins. Do a regular stitch, working off last 2 loops with new skein. Work 3 or 4 rows to establish tension, then return to beginning and knot new skein to tail of old.

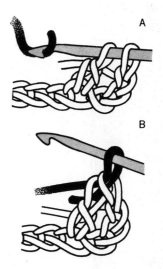

Changing color by working last yarn over (yo) of stitch with second color.

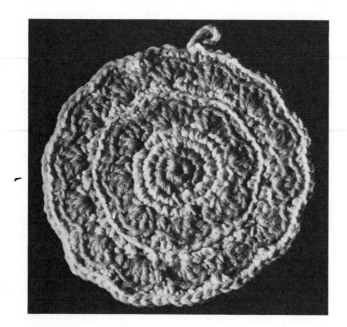

Texture in crochet is produced by the movement of the stitches; textural variation, by the way in which the stitches are combined in a pattern. On this and the following pages are patterns of different combinations—lace, cluster, raised, and twisted (others can be found in projects throughout the book). *Note:* When practicing patterns, make starting chain long enough to accommodate at least 3 pattern repeats.

shell

A group of 3 or more stitches worked in one stitch.

Multiple of 6 + 1 ch.

Row 1: 2 dc in 4th ch from hook (half shell made), * sk 2 ch, sc in next ch, sk 2 ch, 5 dc in next ch (shell made—see diag.). Rep from *, ending sk 2 ch, sc in last ch. Ch 3, turn.

Row 2: 2 dc in first sc of pr r, * sc in 3rd dc of shell, 5 dc in next sc. Rep from *, ending sc in top of turning ch-3. Ch 3, turn.

Rep row 2 for pattern.

filet mesh

An openwork pattern with many design variations.

Chain an even number.

Row 1: Dc in 4th ch from hook, * ch 1, sk 1 ch, dc in next ch, rep from * across. Ch 1, turn.

Row 2: Sc in first st, * sc in next ch-1 sp, sc in next dc, rep from * across. Ch 4, turn.

Row 3: Dc in 3rd st, * ch 1, sk 1 st, dc in next st, rep from * across. Ch 1, turn.

Rep rows 2 and 3 for pattern, ending with row 2.

open shell

A lacy variation of the basic shell.

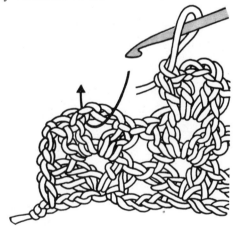

Multiple of 6 + 4 ch.

Row 1: Work (2 dc, ch 3, 2 dc) in 6th ch from hook (open shell made), * sk next 5 ch (2 dc, ch 3, 2 dc) in next ch. Rep from * across, ending sk 3 ch, dc in last ch. Ch 3, turn.

Row 2: * (2 dc, ch 3, 2 dc) in next ch-3 sp (see diag.). Rep from * across, ending dc in top of turning ch-3. Ch 3, turn.

Rep row 2 for pattern.

cluster

Two or more stitches gathered into a group.

Multiple of 3 + 1 ch.

Row 1: In 4th ch from hook work (yo and draw through a lp, yo and through 2 lps) twice, yo and through the 3 lps on hook (beg cluster made), * ch 2, sk 2 ch, (yo, insert hook in next ch, yo, draw through a lp, yo, and through 2 lps) 3x, yo and through the 4 lps on hook—see diag. (cluster made). Rep from * across. Ch. 3, turn.

Row 2: (Yo, insert hook in top of cl of pr r, draw through a lp, yo and through 2 lps) twice, yo and through the 3 lps on hook, * ch 2, make a cl in next cl of pr r. Rep from * across. Ch 3, turn.

Rep row 2 for pattern.

puff

A cluster stitch variation in a closed pattern.

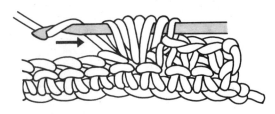

Multiple of 4 ch.

Row 1: (right side) Sc in 2nd ch from hook, * sc in next ch. Rep from * across. Ch 1, turn.

Row 2: Sc in first 3 sts, * yo, insert hook into next st, yo, draw through a lp (yo, insert into same st, yo, draw through a lp) 2x, yo and through the 7 lps on hook (diag.). One puff st made. Sc in each of next 3 sc, rep from * across. Ch 1, turn.

Row 3: Sc in each st across, ch 1, turn.

Row 4: Sc in first st, * puff st in next st, sc in each of next 3 sts. Rep from * across. Ch 1, turn.

Row 5: Sc in each st across. Ch 1, turn.

Rep rows 2–5 for pattern.

popcorn

This stitch gathers a shell into a fat cluster.

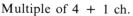

Multiple of 4 + 1 ch.

Row 1: (right side) Dc in 4th from hook, ch 1, 5 dc in next ch, remove hook from lp, insert hook, *front to back,* in top of first dc of 5-dc group, draw dropped lp through first dc (diag.), ch 1 to tighten (popcorn made), * dc in each of next 3 ch, popcorn in next ch. Rep from * across. Ch 3, turn.

Row 2: Dc in 2nd st (turning ch-3 counts as first dc), dc in next st, * ch 1, 5 dc in top of next popcorn of pr r, remove hook from lp, insert hook, *back to front,* in first dc of 5-dc group, draw dropped lp through first dc, ch 1 to tighten (popcorn made on right side), dc in each of next 3 dc. Rep from * across. Ch 3, turn.

Row 3: Rep row 2, except insert hook *front to back* for popcorn.

Rep rows 2 and 3 for pattern.

crossed double crochet

A stitch with a twist in an alternating pattern.

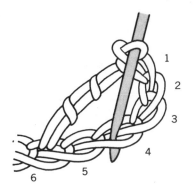

Chain an even number.

Row 1: Dc in 6th ch from hook (the first 3 chs count as first dc), ch 1; crossing over dc just made, dc in 4th ch from beg (diag.), * sk 2 ch, dc in next ch, ch 1; crossing over dc just made, dc in first ch of sk-2 ch. Rep from *, ending dc in last ch. Ch 4, turn.

Row 2: Sk first 2 dc, dc in next dc, ch 1, dc in last skipped dc, * sk dc, ch 1, dc in next dc, ch 1, dc in skipped dc. Rep from *, ending dc in 3rd ch of turning ch-4.

Rep row 2 for pattern.

solomon's knot

An open, long stitch, resembling netting.

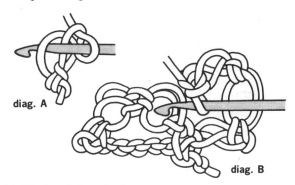

Multiple of 5 + 2 ch.

Row 1: Sc in 2nd ch from hook, * pull up lp on hook until it is ¾″ long, yo, draw through a lp (making a long ch st), insert hook between lp and single strand of ch **(diag. A)** and work sc (single knot st made). Rep from * once more (double knot st made), sk next 4 ch, sc in next ch (knot completed). Rep from first * across, ending with 1 double and 2 single knot sts.

Row 2: * Sc in long lp of first knot st of pr r **(diag. B),** sc in long lp of 2nd knot st, work a double knot st. Rep from * across, ending with 1 double and 2 single knot sts.

Rep row 2 for pattern.

GRANNY SQUARE

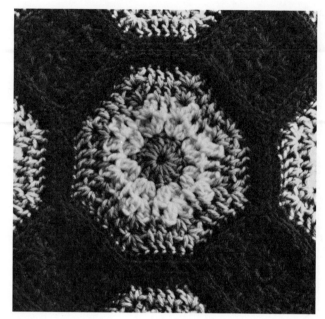

OCTAGON SWIRL

Motifs

Each symetrically-designed motif is a complete unit in itself, yet becomes a related part of the whole when joined with other motifs to form finished pieces. Motifs can also be used individually as decorative additions. *Note:* Do not turn. Always work with right side facing you.

granny square

Worked with four colors: A, B, C, D.

With A, ch 6, join with sl st to form ring (page 17 or 24). ·

Rnd 1: Ch 3, work 2 dc in ring, ch 2, work (3 dc in ring, ch 2)3x. Join with sl st to top of ch-3. Fasten off.

Rnd 2: Attach B in any ch-2 sp, ch 3, (2 dc, ch 2, 3 dc) in same ch-2 sp, ch 1, * (3 dc, ch 2, 3 dc) in next ch-2 sp, ch 1, rep from * twice more. Join with sl st to top of ch-3. Fasten off.

Rnd 3: Attach C in any ch-2 sp, ch 3, (2 dc, ch 2, 3 dc) in same ch-2 sp, ch 1, 3 dc in next ch-1 sp, ch 1, * (3 dc, ch 2, 3 dc) in next ch-2 sp, ch 1, 3 dc in next ch-1 sp, ch 1, rep from * twice more. Join with sl st to top of ch-3. Fasten off.

Rnd 4: Attach D in any ch-2 sp, ch 3, (2 dc, ch 2, 3 dc) in same ch-2 sp, ch 1, (3 dc in next ch-1 sp, ch 1)2x, * (3 dc, ch 2, 3 dc) in next ch-2 sp, ch 1, (3 dc in next ch-1 sp, ch 1)2x, rep from * twice more. Join with sl st to top of ch-3. Fasten off.

octagon swirl

Worked with four colors, A, B, C, D.

With A, ch 6, join with sl st to form ring.

Rnd 1: Ch 3, work 15 dc in ring. Join with sl st to top of ch-3. Break off.

Rnd 2: Attach B to any st, (ch 3, 1 dc, ch 1, 2 dc) in same st, sk 1 st, * (2 dc, ch 1, 2 dc) in next st, sk 1 st, rep from * 6 more times (8 groups). Join to top of ch-3.

Rnd 3: Sl st across first dc to ch-1 sp, (ch 3, 1 dc, ch 1, 2 dc) in same sp, dc in sk-1 sp of pr r, * (2 dc, ch 1, 2 dc) in next ch-1 sp, dc in next sk-1 sp, rep from * 7 more times. Join to top of ch-3. Break off.

Rnd 4: Attach C to any ch-1 sp, (ch 3, 1 dc, ch 1, 2 dc) in same sp, sk 2 sts, 1 dc in each of next 2 sps, * (2 dc, ch 1, 2 dc) in next ch-1 sp, dc in each of next 2 sps (before and after dc of pr r), rep from * around. Join to top of ch-3.

Rnd 5: Sl st across first dc to ch-1 sp, (ch 3, 1 dc, ch

CIRCLE IN SQUARE

1, 2 dc) in same ch-1 sp, sk 2 sts, 1 dc in each of next 3 sps, * (2 dc, ch 1, 2 dc) in next ch-1 sp, sk 2 sts, 1 dc in each of next 3 sps, rep from * around. Join to top of ch-3. Break off.

Rnd 6: Attach D to any st, ch 1, work 1 hdc in each st around and 2 hdc in each ch-1 sp. Join to first st. Fasten off.

circle in square

Ch 8, join with sl st to form ring.

Rnd 1: Ch 5 (counts as first dc and ch 2), * 1 dc in ring, ch 2, rep from * 10 more times, ending sl st in 3rd ch of ch-5. (12 dc)

Rnd 2: Ch 3, dc in *back* loop of each st and ch around, ending sl st in top of ch-3. (36 dc)

Rnd 3: Ch 7 (counts as first dc and ch 4), sk 2 sts, * dc in *back* loop of next st, ch 4, sk 2 sts, rep from * around, ending sl st in 3rd ch of ch-7. (12 dc)

Rnd 4: Sl st in ch-4 sp of pr r, ch 4 (counts as first tr), 4 tr in same sp, ch 1, * 5 tr in next ch-4 sp, ch 1, rep from * around, ending sl st in 4th ch of ch-4. (60 tr)

Rnd 5: Ch 11 (counts as first tr and ch 7), sk 5 tr, * 1 tr in next ch-1 sp, ch 7, sk 5 tr, rep from * around, ending sl st in 4th ch of ch-11. (12 tr)

Rnd 6: Ch 1, sc in *back* loop of every st and ch around, ending sl st in first st. (96 sc)

Rnd 7: *Ch 7, sk 7 sts, hdc in next st, ch 1, dc in next st, ch 1, tr in next st, ch 7, sk 3 sts, tr in next st, ch 1, dc in next st, ch 1, hdc in next st, ch 7, sk 7 sts, sc in next st, rep from * around. (4 corners formed.) End sl st in first ch. Fasten off.

working geometric shapes

By following the instructions given here, you will be able to make any geometric shape. Variations on some of these basic methods will be found in the motifs above and in projects throughout the book.

Square. Begin with a ring and work in a multiple of 4 sts, including incs. Shape square by dividing work into fourths, so that, for example, a rnd of 12 sts would divide into 4 groups of 3 sts each. You would then * work 1 st in each of next 2 sts, 3 sts into 3rd st (corner made), rep from * around. Join with sl st to beg st. Continue working evenly and putting 3 sts into one st at every corner.

A *Hexagon* is worked in a multiple of 6 sts. Shape by dividing work into sixths and putting 3 sts into every 6th st. An *Octagon* is worked in a multiple of 8 sts.

Oval. Make a ch (its length will be the difference between length and width of planned piece; for example, a 4″ x 6″ piece would start on a 2″ ch). Work one st in each ch across, ending with 3 sts in last ch. Do not turn work, but continue along bottom edge of ch, in top loop *only,* ending with 2 sts in last ch. Join with sl st to first st. Continue working, as in a round; inc by 3 sts at each end. As oval grows in size, inc further on curves to keep the work flat. Ch when needed.

Diamond, Triangle. Making diamonds and making triangles are really exercises in inc and dec. *For diamond:* ch 2 and work 2 sts in 2nd ch from hook, ch 1, turn. For next row work 2 sts in each of the 2 sts, ch 1, turn. Inc in first and last st of each row for desired width, then dec in first and last st of every row. Continue in this manner. *For triangle:* Work one half of diamond as above. Or start on a long ch and dec until only 2 or 3 sts remain.

Finishings

After your work is completed you may want to consider the following finishing touches—all of which are simple to do. The picots and reverse sc are trims to outline the work; they are crocheted into the edge of the finished piece. The small designs of the picots make them also suitable as insertions. The double ch, made separately and then sewn on, is used as cording, as a substitute for braids, or as a belt tie. It also provides a strong foundation to build work onto. Fringes, tassels, and pompons are versatile decorations that can be attached singly or in profusion. Finishings are sometimes worked in different yarn weights and color for emphasis.

Simple Picot

SIMPLE PICOT

Attach yarn. With right side facing, sl st in first 2 sts, * sc in next st, ch 3, sc in same st as first sc, sl st in next 2 sts, rep from *.

PICOT

Attach yarn. With right side facing, sc in first st, * ch 5, sl st in 4th ch from hook, ch 1, sk next st, sc in next st, rep from *.

Picot

REVERSE SC

Attach yarn. Work 1 row sc, ch 1, *but do not turn,* insert hook from front into first st to right of hook (diag.) and work a sc, * sc in next st to right of st just made, rep from *.

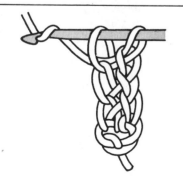

DOUBLE CH OR CH OF SC

Ch 2, sc in 2nd ch from hook, * insert hook under single top strand at *left* edge of last sc made (diag.), yo and draw through a loop (2 loops on hook), yo and through the 2 loops on hook, rep from * for desired length.

FRINGE

Wind yarn around cardboard cut 1″ longer than desired length of fringe (extra inch is for knot takeup) and cut along one edge. Insert hook into fabric, pick up the doubled strands of one group and pull through, forming a loop. Pull ends through loop, knotting them. Another row of knots can be added by knotting the halves of adjacent groups together.

A four-strand ribbon fringe drawn through crocheted edge.

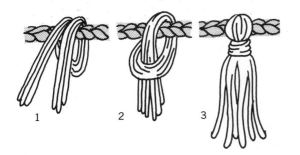

TASSEL

Wind yarn around cardboard cut to desired length of tassel. The number of times yarn is wound around depends on how plump you wish to make tassel. Insert an extra length of yarn through one end of group and tie securely. This length will be used to tie tassel to fabric. Cut strands at other end. Tightly wrap a second strand a few times around group, ½″ to 1″ below first, and knot it. Tie tassel around edge loop, sew down, and trim ends.

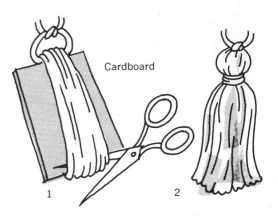

POMPON

Cut cardboard circles to desired size of pompon and cut a hole about ¼″ in center of each—or purchase plastic circles (they come in various sizes). Cut 4 lengths of yarn, each 3 yds. long. Place circles together and wind yarn around, drawing it through center and over edges. Continue until circles are completely covered and opening is filled in. Cut yarn along outside edges. Slip a length of yarn between the cardboards and wind it around very tightly several times; secure with a knot, leaving ends long enough to fasten pompon to fabric. Tear cardboards away. Fluff pompon and trim.

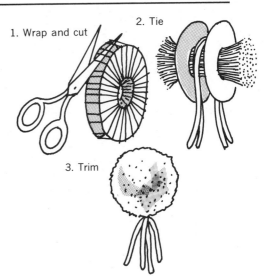

Tote Bags

The special feature of the tote bags shown on the facing page and on page 38 is the attractive use of unusual materials—sisal twine and plastic lanyard. Such materials produce sturdy, practical items that are relatively care free. The sisal tote is made in rounds: its base in single crochet, its sides in filet mesh. It can also be used as a decorative basket or a planter. The lanyard tote is worked with the open V stitch and is made in two sections that are later joined.

Base of sisal tote worked in rounds of single crochet.

Detail of filet mesh stitches worked on sides of sisal tote.

sisal tote bag or planter 11″ deep, 11″ diameter

Materials: #1 sisal twine, 600 ft. or approx. 32 oz. J crochet hook.

Gauge: 2 sc = 1″; 4 rows = 3″

PATTERN STITCH: Sc and filet mesh in rounds.

Ch 4, join with sl st to form ring.

Rnd 1: Ch 1, work 8 sc in ring. Join with sl st to first st.

Rnd 2: Ch 1, work 2 sc in each st around (16 sts). Join with sl st to first st.

Rnd 3: Ch 1, * 2 sc in next st, sc in next st, rep from * around (24 sts). Join with sl st to first st.

Rnd 4: Ch 1, * sc in each of next 2 sts, 2 sc in next st, rep from * around (32 sts). Join with sl st to first st.

Rnd 5: Ch 1, * 2 sc in next st, sc in each of next 3 sts, rep from * around (40 sts). Join.

Rnds 6–9: Continue to inc 8 sts evenly around for 4 more rounds (72 sts). For example: row 6 is worked, sc in each of next 4 sts, 2 sc in next st. Try not to put incs directly above each other. Base of tote bag or planter completed.

Rnds 10 & 11: Ch 1, work sc in each st around. Join.

Rnd 12: (Filet mesh) Ch 4, * sk 1 st, dc in next st, ch 1, rep from * around. Join with sl st to 3rd ch of ch-4.

Rnd 13: Ch 1, sc in st just joined, * sc in next ch-1 sp of pr r, sc in next dc, rep from * around. Join with sl st to first st.

Rep rows 12 and 13 until piece is 11″ high, ending with row 13.

Fasten off, weave in ends. For tote bag, insert a handle—either crocheted or purchased—through filet mesh spaces. A nylon nautical rope, ½″ in diameter, was used here.

Tote bag, 11″ deep, 11″ diameter, made with sisal twine. Shown right with thick nylon rope handle and below as planter.

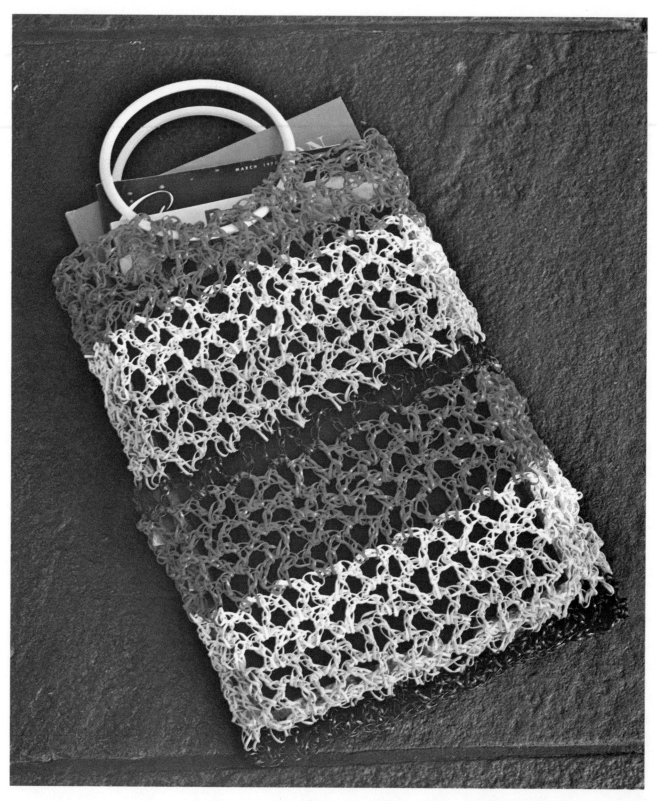

Tote bag, 14″ x 18″, in three colors, made with plastic lanyard in the V stitch.

lanyard tote bag 14" x 18"

Materials: American Handicrafts, Dura-Flex vinyl corded lace.
J crochet hook. Circular handbag handles.
100 yds. orange   50 yds. white
75 yds. yellow   25 yds. green

Gauge: 1 V st = 1"; 1 row = 1"

PATTERN STITCH: V stitch. Multiple of 3 + 6 ch.

First side: With green, ch 39.

Row 1: Dc in 6th ch from hook, * sk 2 ch, (dc, ch 2, dc) in next ch (V st made), rep from * across. Work last yo and draw through 2 lps with yellow (*Note:* All color changes are done in this manner—working last yo and drawing through new color). Break off green. With yellow, ch 5, turn.

Row 2: Dc in first ch-2 sp, *(dc, ch 2, dc) in next ch-2 sp, rep from * across, ending (dc, ch 2, dc) in lp of ch-5. Ch 5, turn.

Rep row 2 for pattern and change colors as follows:

3 rows yellow   3 rows yellow
2 rows white   2 rows white
4 rows orange   4 rows orange
1 row green

Fasten off. Rep for second side. To finish: Weave sides tog. Sl st tog at bottom. Weave in ends. Place handles at top center of each half, fold each top of tote bag over a handle, and sew in place.

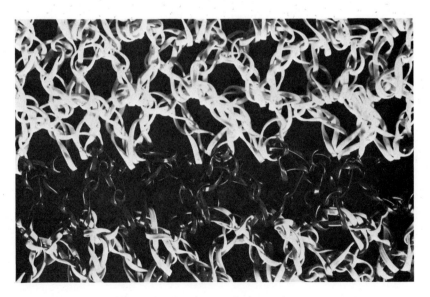

Detail of V stitch. Shown in the three colors used.

Stoles and Shawl

Two stoles and one shawl—light, soft, and lacy but different texturally because of the stitches used. The pink stole (pictured on page 43) uses the afghan stitch with cluster, a combination that creates a circular effect in the design. The white shawl (facing page), made of fluffy mohair, is in the single knot stitch (the first half of Solomon's knot) and results in a delicate looped lace. The yellow stole (pictured on page 43) is made in single crochet pulled long and worked over a cardboard strip for a linear pattern. As with all projects in this book, change colors to suit your needs.

Detail of pink stole showing clusters formed in afghan stitch rows.

pink stole 18″ x 68″ (excluding fringe)

Materials: Bernat & Co., Barella sport yarn, six 2-oz. skeins.
10 afghan hook.

Gauge: one cluster = 1″

PATTERN STITCH: Lace afghan st with cluster (cl). Mult of 4 + 1 ch. *Note:* Each afghan row is worked in 2 steps (page 18 or 25). *Do not turn work throughout.*

Ch 89 loosely.

Row 1:

A. *Keeping all loops on hook,* pick up a lp in top lp *only* of 2nd ch from hook and in each ch across. (89 lps)

B. *Working loops off hook,* * ch 3, yo and draw through 5 lps on hook (cl made), yo and draw through one lp to tighten cl, rep from * across. One lp remains on hook. At end of row, ch 1.

Row 2:

A. Pick up a lp in top of each cl and in top lp of each ch of ch-3 across.

B. Same as row 1B.

Rep row 2 until piece measures 68″, ending sl st in top of each cl and in top lp of each ch of ch-3 across. Fasten off.

To finish: With right side facing, attach yarn to starting ch and sl st in each ch across. Weave in ends. Block. Make a 5″ fringe; attach 4 doubled strands in every 4th sl st across each end of stole.

mohair shawl 66″ x 33″ (excluding fringe)

Materials: Columbia Minerva Reverie, ten 1-oz balls.
F crochet hook.

Gauge: 4 knots sts = 3″; 7 rows = 3″

PATTERN STITCH: Single knot st. Chain is an even number.

Ch 150 loosely.

Row 1: Sc in 2nd ch from hook, * pull up lp on hook until it is ½″ long, yo and draw through a lp (long ch st made), insert hook between lp and single strand of ch **(diag. A,** page 31), and work 1 sc (single knot st made), sk 1 ch, sc in next ch, rep from * across. Ch 1, turn.

Row 2: Sc in long lp of first knot st of pr r (knot st dec made), * make a knot st, sc in next long lp st of pr r, rep from * across. Ch 1, turn.

Rep row 2 until 6 knot sts remain. Fasten off, weave in ends. To finish, attach yarn to starting ch, work sc across. Fasten off. Make a 6″ fringe; attach 4 doubled strands in each knot st around all edges but top edge.

VARIATION: If you want a rectangular-shaped shawl, rather than a triangular one, ch more sts on to start, work row 1, and change pattern row 2 as follows:

Sc in first sc of pr r, * make a knot st, sc in next long loop of pr r, rep from * across. Ch 1, turn.

White shawl made with mohair in the single knot stitch.

Detail of white shawl showing single knot stitch (first half of Solomon's knot).

yellow stole 22" x 72"

Materials: Knitting worsted, 12 oz: J crochet hook.
2 cardboard strips, 1½" and 3" wide; any length.

Gauge: 5 sc = 2"

PATTERN STITCH: Long sc. Chain is an even number.

Ch 180 loosely.

Row 1: Sc in 2nd ch from hook and in each ch across. Ch 1, turn.

Row 2: (Long sc) Pull up lp on hook to height of 1½" cardboard strip, place strip in front of lp. Working over strip, insert hook in first st, yo, pull up lp to top of strip, yo and through 2 lps on hook (long sc made), ch 1, sk next st, * long sc in next st, ch 1, sk next st, rep from * across. Ch 1, turn. Slide strip out of lps.

Row 3: Sc in first ch, sc in long sc, * sc in next ch, sc in next long sc, rep from * across. Ch 1, turn.

Row 4: Sc in each sc across.

Rep rows 2 and 3 for pattern, working row 2 once more with 1½" strip, then 5 times with 3" strip. Fasten off, weave in ends. Block. Add fringe if desired.

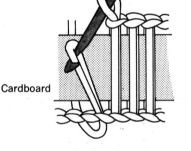

Cardboard

Long single crochet. Yarn pulled up to height of cardboard to make chain stitch. Cardboard rests on top of previous row. Hold work in whatever position is most comfortable.

Detail of yellow stole. Note how the long single crochet stitches are held secure between rows of single crochet.

(Above) Pink stole made with sport yarn in afghan and cluster stitches.

(Right) Yellow stole made with knitting worsted in long single crochet.

Placemats and Casement

The pieces in this section are good examples of how basic stitches can combine with the chain stitch to make a pattern. In all of the following, the chain stitch contributes greatly toward the final pattern. The blue placemat below combines single, double, and triple crochet to produce an original radial design. The green placemat on page 47 combines single and double crochet and results in picots and a knobby texture. The pink placemat on page 47, with the Circle in Square motif (page 33), combines double and triple crochet and is worked in sections. The pink-red placemat (page 47) is double crochet throughout. The casement (page 46) is made by varying the pattern of the pink-red placemat slightly.

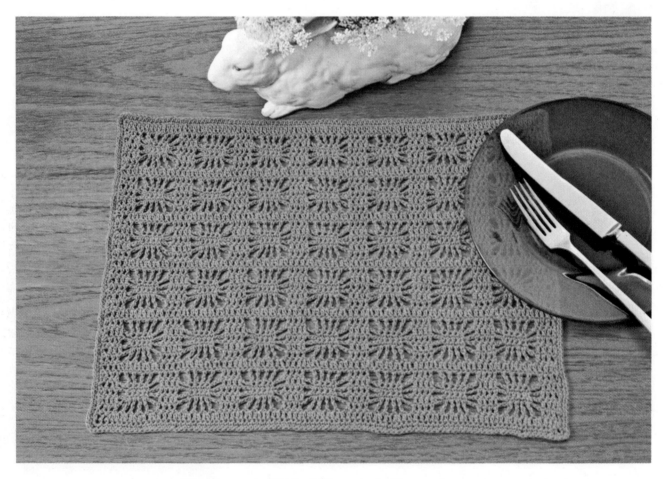

Blue placemat, 16½'' x 12'', worked with carpet warp.

four designs for placemats

PATTERN #1: Multiple of 13 + 6 ch.

Row 1: Dc in 4th ch from hook and in each ch across. Ch 3, turn.

Row 2: (Turning ch-3 counts as first dc) Dc in 2nd st, dc in each of next 2 sts, * ch 3, (sk 1 st, tr in next st) 4x, ch 3, sk 1 st, dc in each of next 4 sts, rep from * across. Ch 3, turn.

Row 3: Dc in 2nd st, dc in each of next 2 sts, * ch 3, sc in each of next 4 tr, ch 3, dc in each of next 4 dc, rep from * across. Ch 3, turn.

Rows 4 & 5: Dc in 2nd st, dc in each of next 2 sts, * ch 3, sc in each of next 4 sc, ch 3, dc in each of next 4 dc, rep from * across. Ch 3, turn.

Row 6: Dc in 2nd st, dc in each of next 2 sts, * (ch 1, tr) in each of next 4 sc, ch 1, dc in each of next 4 dc, rep from * across. Ch 3, turn.

Row 7: Dc in 2nd st, dc in each st and ch across. Ch 3, turn.

Rep rows 2 to 7 for pattern.

TWO BLUE PLACEMATS, each 16½″ x 12″: Lily Tru-Tone carpet warp, 400-yd. spool. #1 steel crochet hook. Gauge: 6 dc = 1″; 3 rows = 1″. Ch 97, work row 1. Work pat rows 6x. Fasten off. Attach yarn, work 2 rows sc around, 3 sc in each corner. Fasten off.

PATTERN #2: Picot lace. Multiple of 7 + 4 ch.

Row 1: Hdc in 3rd ch from hook, hdc in next ch, * ch 3, sk 2 ch, sc in next ch, ch 3, sk 2 ch, hdc in each of next 2 ch, rep from * across. Ch 2, turn.

Row 2: Hdc in each of first 2 hdc, * ch 3, (1 sc, ch 3, 1 sc) in next sc, ch 3, hdc in each of next 2 hdc, rep from * across. Ch 1, turn.

Row 3: Sc in each of first 2 hdc, * sc in ch-3 sp, ch 5, sc in next ch-3 sp, sc in each of next 2 hdc, rep from * across. Ch 1, turn.

Row 4: Sc in each of first 2 sc, * 7 sc in ch-5 sp (arch), sk 1 sc, sc in each of next 2 sc, rep from * across. Ch 2, turn.

Row 5: Hdc in each of first 2 sc, * ch 3, sk 3 sc, sc in next sc, ch 3, sk 3 sc, hdc in each of next 2 sc, rep from * across. Ch 2, turn.

Rep rows 2 to 5 for pattern.

GREEN LINEN PLACEMAT, 17½″ x 12½″: Fredrick J. Fawcett's 10/2 linen, 3 oz. #7 steel crochet hook. Gauge: 3 pat reps across = 4″. Ch 95, work row 1. Work pat rows until piece measures 12″, end with row 5. Fasten off. Finish with 1 row sc around, 3 sc in each ch-3 sp, 3 sc in each corner. Join. Work 1 row reverse sc around.

PATTERN #3: See Circle in Square, page 33.

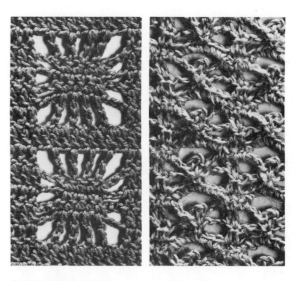

(Left) Detail of blue placemat showing triple crochet in a radial pattern. (Right) Detail of green placemat showing picot loops.

Detail of pink placemat (see page 47). Note how motifs are joined.

(Above) Casement. A variation of pink-red placemat pattern turned vertically for hanging. (Below) Detail of above pattern shows long chains gathered in the center by single crochet stitches.

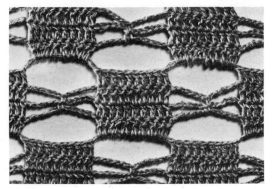

PINK PLACEMAT, 16½″ x 11½″: Unger's Erica (cotton/linen), two 1-oz. skeins. E crochet hook. Work 6 motifs, each = 5¼″ square. Block, sew tog, 3 across, 2 down. Attach yarn to any ch-7 corner, work 5 sc in corner sp, 1 sc in each st around, 1 sc in each ch-1 sp, 5 sc in each ch-7 corner sp. Join to first st. Next row: Ch 3, dc in 2nd st, 3 dc in next st (corner), * dc in each st around, 3 dc in each corner st, rep from * around. Fasten off.

PATTERN #4: Multiple of 20 + 12 ch.

Row 1: Dc in 4th ch from hook and in each of next 8 ch, * ch 10, sk 10 ch, dc in each of next 10 ch, rep from * across. Ch 3, turn.

Row 2: Dc in 2nd st (ch-3 counts as first dc), dc in each of next 8 sts, * ch 5, sc in ch-10 sp, ch 5, dc in each of next 10 dc, rep from * across. Ch 3, turn.

Row 3: Rep row 2, except change "sc in ch-10 sp" to sc in sc of pr r.

Row 4: Dc in 2nd st and in each of next 8 sts, * ch 10, dc in each of next 10 dc, rep from * across. Turn.

Row 5: Ch 13, * 10 dc in ch-10 sp, ch 10, rep from *, ending dc in last dc of pr r. Turn.

Row 6: Ch 8, sc in ch-10 sp, ch 5, * dc in each of next 10 dc, ch 5, sc in ch-10 sp, ch 5, rep from *, ending dc in 11th ch of ch-13.

Row 7: Rep row 6, except change "sc in ch-10 sp" to sc in sc of pr r. End row with dc in 6th ch of ch-8. Turn.

Row 8: Ch 13, * dc in each of next 10 dc, ch 10, rep from *, ending dc in top of ch-13. Ch 3, turn.

Row 9: 9 dc in ch-10 sp, * ch 10, 10 dc in next ch-10 sp, rep from * across. Ch 3, turn.

Rep rows 2 to 9 for pattern.

FOUR PINK-RED PLACEMATS, each 16″ x 13″: Unger's Erica (cotton/linen), nine 1-oz. skeins. E crochet hook. Gauge: 5 dc = 1″; 3 rows = 1″. Ch 72, work row 1. Work pat rows until piece measures 12″, end with row 8. Fasten off. Finish with 1 row sc around, 8 sc in ch-10 sps. Block. Make 4 tassels, each 2″ long, and attach.

CASEMENT (a variation on pattern #4). 10/2 linen, 2 oz. B crochet hook. Gauge: 6 dc = 1″; 5 rows = 2″. Multiple of 22 + 12 ch.

Ch 144 to start. 7 pat reps = 26″ x 22″; further reps will add to width. To add to length, ch more to start or work separate pieces, then join. Follow pat #4 directions except inc all ch 5 and ch 8 by one ch, inc all other chs (except turning chs) by 2 chs. Row 1, for example, would be: Dc in 4th ch from hook and in each of next 8 ch, * ch 12, sk 12 ch, dc in each of next 10 ch, rep from * across. Finish same as placemat, minus tassels.

(Above) Green placemat, 17½'' x 12½'', worked with 10/2 linen. (See page 45.)

(Right) Pink placemat, 16½'' x 11½'', Circle in Square motif.

(Below) Pink-red placemat, 16'' x 13'', worked with variegated yarn.

Pillow Covers

The traditional granny square makes a good beginner's project. It is used in the pillow covers on this page in two different color combinations. The colors to the left, below, are placed in the same order throughout, whereas the ones below right are alternated. The rich surface of the pillow covers is the result of brilliant hues and velvety soft chenille yarn. The pinwheel pillow cover (facing page) uses the afghan stitch, thus creating a flat surface that does not conflict with the contemporary design—a design in which bands of color, diamonds, and other geometric forms combine to give variety of shape. All the covers are worked in separate motifs that are joined at the finish.

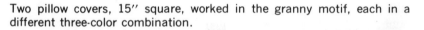

Two pillow covers, 15″ square, worked in the granny motif, each in a different three-color combination.

Pinwheel pillow cover, 15″ square, worked in the afghan stitch. Eight
sections are made, four for each side.

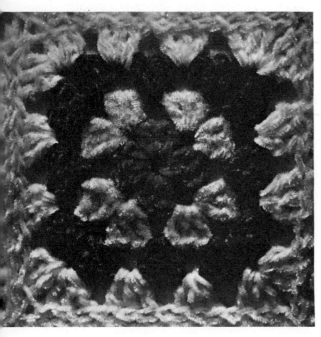

Granny motif, 5″ square.

2	3	2
3	1	3
2	3	2

Color positions for Red, Pink, and White pillow cover.

granny pillow covers

Both pillow covers use Fibre Yarn Co. chenille yarn. H crochet hook.

PATTERN STITCH: Granny square, follow directions on page 32. Each motif = 5″ square.

YELLOW, ORANGE, AND GREEN PILLOW COVER, 15″ x 15″: Make 18 squares using the following yarn amounts:

135 ft. light yellow (color A)   297 ft. orange (color C)
198 ft. yellow (color B)   405 ft. green (color D)

Weave in all ends at finish. Weave squares together, 3 across, 6 down. Fold work in half and weave tog on 2 sides, leaving one side open for pillow insertion. Insert pillow and sew opening closed. Either use a purchased pillow or make your own by cutting 2 pieces of fabric 17″ square, seaming them together on three sides and stuffing with Kapok or shredded foam. Sew remaining side closed. For a variation, make squares for front of pillow only and finish the back with velveteen or other material.

RED, PINK, AND WHITE PILLOW COVER, 15″ x 15″. Make 18 squares using the following yarn amounts:

235 ft. dark red (color A)   181 ft. pink (color C)
214 ft. red (color B)   405 ft. white (color D)

1. Make 2 squares, working rnd 1 in color A, rnd 2 in color B, rnd 3 in color C, rnd 4 in color D. (Square 1)

2. Make 8 squares, working rnd 1 in color B, rnd 2 in color C, rnd 3 in color A, rnd 4 in color D. (Square 2)

3. Make 8 squares, working rnd 1 in color C, rnd 2 in color A, rnd 3 in color B, rnd 4 in color D. (Square 3)

Weave in ends. To finish, weave 9 squares together for front, placing A square in the center, B squares in each corner, and C squares in remaining areas. Rep for back. Weave 3 sides together, leaving one open for pillow insertion. Insert; sew opening closed.

pinwheel pillow cover 15″ x 15″

Materials: Knitting worsted. #2 afghan hook.
4 oz. turquoise   2 oz. white
4 oz. purple   2 oz. black
4 oz. medium blue 2 oz. red
2 oz. gold

Gauge: 6 sts = 1″; 5 rows = 1″

PATTERN STITCH: Afghan stitch. Make 8 motifs in all. *Note:* Each row is worked in 2 steps (page 18 or 25). *Do not turn work throughout.*

TO MAKE MOTIF A: With turquoise, ch 40.

Row 1:

A. (Draw through a lp in top lp *only* of 2nd ch from hook and in each ch across.) Draw through first 5 ch with turquoise, next 3 ch with white, next 31 ch with turquoise.

B. With turquoise, yo and through 1 lp on hook, * yo and through 2 lps on hook, rep from * 30x with turquoise, 3x with white, 5x with turquoise, once with purple.

Row 2:

A. Draw up a lp in 2nd vertical bar with turquoise, * draw up a lp in next vertical bar, rep from * 5x with turquoise, 3x with white, 29x with turquoise, once with black.

B. With black, yo and through 1 lp on hook, change to turquoise, * yo and through 2 lps on hook, rep from * 28 more times with turquoise, 3x with white, 6x with turquoise, once with purple.

Rows 3–34: Follow color changes on graph.

At end, sl st in each vertical bar across in matching color.

Make two A motifs.

TO MAKE MOTIFS B, C, D: Make two of each. Follow graph for color changes.

To finish, join motifs for each pillow half as shown. Sew 3 sides tog, leaving one side open for pillow insertion. Insert and sew closed.

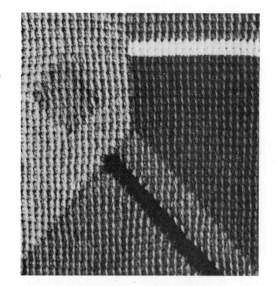

Pinwheel design. One section shown. Other sections are in same design, but different colors. See graph below.

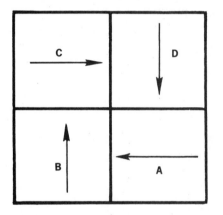

Position the sections as indicated by arrows, then join. Repeat for other side of pillow.

GRAPH AND COLORS FOR PINWHEEL DESIGN

Motif A and C	Motif B and D
1. Turquoise	1. Blue
2. White	2. Black
3. Purple	3. Purple
4. Blue	4. Gold
5. Gold (A), Purple (C)	5. Turquoise (B), Red (D)
6. Red	6. White
7. Gold	7. Turquoise
8. Black	8. Red

Note: With exception of diamond color, sections A and D are in the same colors, as are sections B and C.

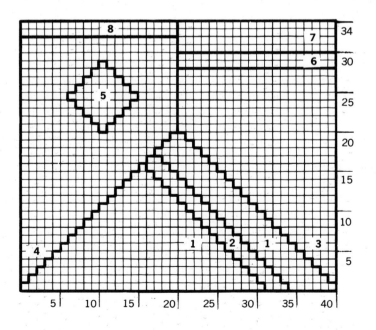

Baby's Blanket and Afghans

The solid-color baby's blanket uses the delicate open shell stitch in an allover pattern. It is ideal for crib or carriage. The basket afghan (pictured on page 54), in a soft, smooth fabric, is worked with alternating colors in the afghan stitch. It is made in four long strips that are later joined. A double granny forms the center of the multi-colored afghan (page 54). This is an ideal project for using up leftover yarn. The star afghan uses two motifs—the Octagon Swirl together with a joining motif. Knitting worsted yarn is used in all.

baby's blanket 36″ x 44″

Materials: Knitting worsted, 20 oz. J crochet hook.

Gauge: 3 shells = 5″

PATTERN STITCH: Lace shell. Multiple of 6 + 2 ch.

Ch 122 loosely.

Row 1: Sc in 2nd ch, sc in next ch, * ch 3, sk 3 ch, sc in each of next 3 ch, rep from *, ending sc in each of last 2 ch. Ch 1, turn.

Row 2: Sc in first st, * 5 dc in ch-3 sp (shell made), sc in 2nd sc, rep from * across. Turn.

Row 3: * Ch 3, 1 sc each in 2nd, 3rd, & 4th dc of shell, rep from *, ending ch 2, sc in last st. Ch 3, turn.

Row 4: 2 dc in ch-2 sp, * sc in 2nd sc, 5 dc in ch-3 sp (shell made), rep from *, ending sc in 2nd sc, 3 dc in ch-3 sp. Ch 1, turn.

Row 5: Sc in each of first 2 dc, * ch 3, 1 sc each in 2nd, 3rd, and 4th dc of shell, rep from *, ending with sc in 2nd dc, sc in top of ch 3, ch 1, turn.

Rep rows 2–5 until piece measures 40″, then work 1 row sc around, 3 sc in each corner. Join with sl st, ch 1. *Do not turn.* Work 1 row hdc, 3 hdc in corners. Join with sl st. Sl st in each st around. Block.

star afghan 66″ x 48″

Materials: Coats & Clark, Red Heart knitting worsted, 4-oz. skeins. G crochet hook.

1 skein dark gold	(color A)
4 skeins white	(color B)
6 skeins blue jewel	(color C)
6 skeins navy	(color D)

Gauge: Each star motif = 6″; each joining motif = 2½″ square

PATTERN STITCH: Octagon Swirl, page 32. Make 88 motifs. Octagons leave spaces when joined; these are filled with joining motifs.

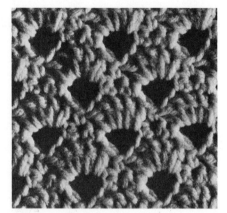

Detail of baby's blanket showing open shell stitch.

Detail of star afghan showing Octagon Swirl motifs and joining motifs.

(Right) Baby's blanket, 36″ x 44″, in open shell stitch.

Star afghan, 66″ x 48″, Octagon Swirl motifs, in knitting worsted, individually made, then joined with a joining motif.

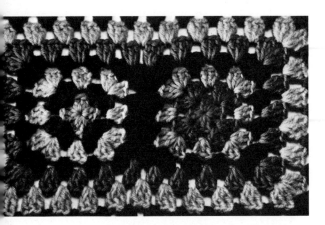

Two granny squares form center of afghan. Design grows row by row around motifs.

JOINING MOTIF: With color D ch 4, join with sl st to form ring.

Rnd 1: Ch 1, work 8 sc in ring. Join with sl st to first st.

Rnd 2: (Ch 3, 2 dc, ch 1, 3 dc) in first st, ch 1, sk 1 st, * (3 dc, ch 1, 3 dc) in next st, ch 1, sk 1 st, rep from * around. Sl st to top of ch-3.

Rnd 3: Sl st across 2 dc to ch-1 sp, (ch 3, 2 dc, ch 1, 3 dc) in same ch-1 sp, 3 dc in next ch-1 sp, * (3 dc, ch 1, 3 dc) in next ch-1 sp, 3 dc in next ch-1 sp, rep from * around. Join with sl st to top of ch-3. Fasten off. Make 70 motifs. Block and join with octagon motifs.

granny afghan 68″ x 62″

Materials: Knitting worsted, approx. sixteen 4-oz. skeins in various colors. J crochet hook.

Gauge: 3 dc = 1″; 3 rows = 1″

Make 2 granny squares, following directions on page 32, and join. Working around squares, do 3 dc in each ch-1 sp and (3 dc, ch 1, 3 dc) in each corner sp. Continue working around in this fashion, changing color each row or in middle of row.

Granny afghan, 68″ x 62″. Made with leftover knitting worsted.

Basket afghan, 48″ square. Made with knitting worsted.

GRAPH FOR BASKET AFGHAN

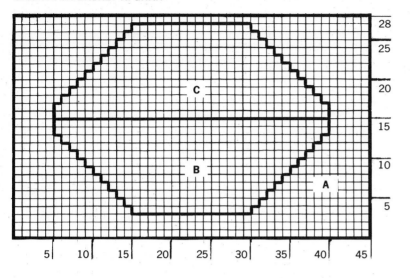

Detail of basket afghan showing how rows are edged. Note that basket colors alternate.

Repeat graph rows for each section. Note that basket colors reverse each time.

basket afghan 48″ x 48″

Materials: Columbia Minerva Nantuk Sweater & Afghan Yarn, 2 oz. skeins. #9 afghan hook. H crochet hook.
 6 skeins dark turquoise (color A)
 6 skeins medium turquoise (color B)
 7 skeins avocado (color C)

Gauge: 5 sts = 1″; 7 rows = 2″

TO MAKE ON STRIP: With C, ch 45. Work rows 1–3 in afghan st.

Row 4:

 A. Draw up a lp in 2nd vertical bar and in each of next 13 bars. Drop C, attach A and draw up a lp in each of next 15 bars, drop A, attach new strand of C and draw up a lp in each of next 15 bars.

 B. Work off lps with C until 2nd lp on hook is color A, change to A and work off 15 sts, change to C and work off remainder of sts.

Rows 5–28: Follow color changes on graph.

Rep rows 1–28 five more times. After last row, work 1 row with C (2nd half of row is sl st in 2nd bar and in each bar across). Fasten off. Make 3 more strips. Block. With A and size H hook, work 1 dc row on long edges of 2 strips (they will form center of afghan). On other 2 strips work dc row only on the long edges that will face inside. Attach B, work 1 dc row on A edges. Sew strips tog along their lengths. Attach A, work 2 dc rows all around, attach B and work 1 dc row. Fasten off.

Potholders

You can have as much fun making these gaily detailed potholders as others will have looking at them. The ladybug, frog, butterfly, and apple are crocheted in rug yarn to insure protection against hot handles. The use of heavy yarn, together with a few simple stitches, insures that the work will go quickly. These are good projects for leftover yarns and for gift-giving.

These potholders were made with Paterneyan Persian rug yarn left over from other projects.

Materials: Approx. one 3½-oz. skein of each color. G crochet hook.

Gauge: 8 sc = 3″; 3 rows = 1″

Note: Abbreviation eon = each of next.

butterfly approx. 8½″ x 7″

Colors: Turquoise (A), pink (B), chartreuse (C), white (D), black (E).

RIGHT WING OF BUTTERFLY: With A, ch 14.

Row 1: (right side) Sc in 2nd ch from hook and in each ch across, ch 1, turn.

Row 2: Sc across, end 2 sc in last st, ch 1, turn.

Row 3: 2 sc in first st, sc in eon 12 sts, 2 sc in last st, ch 1, turn.

Rows 4 & 5: Rep row 2.

Row 6: Sc in each st across, end 1 sc dec (page 16 or 23) in last 2 sts, ch 1, turn.

Row 7: Dec 1 sc, sc in next st and in each st across, end 2 sc in last st, ch 1, turn.

Row 8: Sc in each of first 2 sts, hdc in eon 4 sts, sc in eon 4 sts, sl st across next 2 sts, sc in next st, hdc in next st, dc in eon 2 sts, sc in next st. Fasten off.

(Right side) Attach B to right edge of 5th row, ch 1, 1 hdc on row 6 edge, 1 dc on row 7 edge. On row 8, work 1 dc on edge, 2 hdc in first st, hdc in next st, sc in next st, sl st in next st. Fasten off.

(Right side) Attach C to 3rd B st on right edge, ch 1, sc in next st, hdc in eon 2 sts, sc in next st, sl st in next st. Fasten off.

(Right side) Attach B to 11th A st from left edge, ch 1, sc in eon 4 sts, hdc in eon 4 sts, dc in eon 2 sts. Fasten off.

Attach C in st just before first B st, ch 1, sc in ch-1 of B row, sc in eon 4 sts, hdc in eon 4 sts, dc in eon 2 sts. Fasten off.

LEFT WING OF BUTTERFLY: Rep rows 1 to 8 as for right wing. Row 2 will be right side. With right side facing, attach yarns as before except to left edge.

To finish: Ch 2 with E. With wrong sides facing, join wings with 1 row sc through both A edges. Ch 9 and join ch to last sc for loop. Weave ends. Block. Embroider a circle with D in upper and lower parts of each wing, and one down the center with C.

ladybug 9½″ around

Colors: Red (A), black (B), yellow (C). *Note:* "Work over" yarn for color changes, see page 27.

With A, ch 6, join with sl st to form ring. The first sc of a round is made in the stitch next to the joined stitch. (Round 2 should have 16 sts.)

Rnd 1: Ch 1, 8 sc in center of ring. Join with sl st.

Rnd 2: Ch 1, 2 sc in each st around. Join with sl st.

Rnd 3: Ch 1, * *with A* (sc in next st, 2 sc in next st) 2x, sc in next st, *attach B,* with B work 2 sc in next st, rep from * once more, *with A* (sc in next st, 2 sc in next st) 2x. Join.

Two potholders: apple and frog.

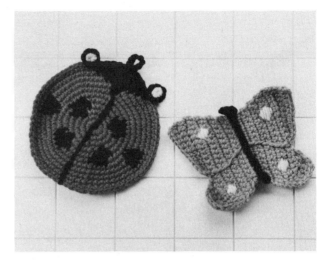

Two potholders: ladybug and butterfly.

Rnd 4: Ch 1, sc in next st. *With B,* 2 sc in next st, *with A* sc in eon 2 sts, 2 sc in next st, *with B* sc in next st, 2 sc in next st, sc in eon 2 sts, *with A* 2 sc in next st, sc in eon 2 sts, 2 sc in next st, sc in next st, *with B* sc in next st, 2 sc in next st, sc in eon 2 sts, *with A* sc in next st, 2 sc in next st, sc in next st, *with B* 2 sc in next st, *with A* sc in next st, 2 sc in next st. Join.

Rnd 5: *With B* ch 1, 2 sc in first st, sc in eon 2 sts, *with A* sc in next st, 2 sc in next st, sc in eon 2 sts, *with B* sc in next st, 2 sc in next st, sc in next st, *with A* sc in eon 2 sts, 2 sc in next st, sc in eon 3 sts, 2 sc in next st, sc in eon 2 sts, *with B* sc in next st, 2 sc in next st, sc in next st, *with A* sc in eon 2 sts, 2 sc in next st, *with B* sc in eon 2 sts, 2 sc in next st, sc in next st, *with A* sc in eon 4 sts. Join *with B.*

Rnd 6: *With B* ch 1, sc in eon 4 sts, *with A* (2 sc, sc in eon 4 sts)5x, 2 sc in next st, sc in eon 2 sts, *with B* sc in eon 4 sts, *with A* 2 sc in next st, sc in eon 4 sts. Join.

Rnd 7: Ch 1, sc in eon 5 sts, *with B* 2 sc in next st, *with A* sc in eon 2 sts, 2 sc in next st, sc in eon 10 sts, *with B* 2 sc in next st, *with A* sc in eon 6 sts, 2 sc in next st, sc in eon 6 sts, *with B* sc in eon 2 sts, *with A* sc in next st, 2 sc in next st, sc in eon 8 sts, 2 sc in next st, sc in eon 2 sts. Join.

Rnd 8: Ch 1, sc in eon 4 sts, *with B* 2 sc in next st, sc in eon 2 sts, *with A* sc in eon 4 sts, 2 sc in next st, sc in eon 8 sts, *with B* 2 sc in next st, sc in eon 2 sts, *with A* sc in eon 7 sts, 2 sc in next st, sc in eon 5 sts, *with B* sc in next st, 2 sc in next st, sc in next st, *with A* sc in eon 8 sts, 2 sc in next st, sc in eon 7 sts. Join.

Rnd 9: Ch 1, sc in eon 4 sts, *with B* 2 sc in next st, sc in eon 2 sts, *with A* sc in eon 13 sts, *with B* sc in eon 7 sts, *with A* sc in eon 12 sts, *with B* sc in eon 4 sts, *with A* sc in eon 18 sts. Join.

Rnd 10: Ch 1, sc in eon 19 sts, *with B* sc in eon 4 sts, 2 sc in next st, sc in eon 5 sts, *with A* sc in eon 33 sts. Join.

Rnd 11: Ch 1, sc in first st, (2 sc in next st, sc in eon 6 sts)2x, sc in next 2 sts, *with B* sl st across next st, sc in eon 2 sts, hdc in eon 7 sts, sc in eon 3 sts, sl st across next st, *with A* sc in next st, (2 sc in next st, sc in eon 7 sts)3x, 2 sc in next st, sc in eon 6 sts. Join. Fasten off.

EYES (make 2): With C ch 2, work 5 dc in 2nd ch from hook, join with sl st. Fasten off. Attach B and sl st in each st around. Fasten off.

To finish: Block. With B embroider a row down the center. Sew an eye at each end of B at top. For loop attach B to center top, ch 9, sl st to beginning. Weave in ends.

frog approx. 8½″ x 7″

Colors: Yellow (A), chartreuse (B), green (C), 1-yd. orange (D).

BODY: With A, ch 16.

Row 1: Hdc in 3rd ch from hook, hdc in eon 5 ch, sc in eon 2 ch, hdc in eon 6 ch. Ch 2, turn.

Rows 2–6: Hdc in each of first 6 sts, sc in eon 2 sts, hdc in eon 6 sts. Ch 2, turn.

Rows 7 & 8: Sk first st (dec), work hdc in hdc and sc in sc across, end sk next to last st (dec).

Row 9: Hdc in each of first 4 sts, sc in eon 2 sts, hdc in eon 4 sts. Fasten off.

HEAD: Ch 4 with B, insert hook in last row of body, work sc in each st across (10 sts), ch 4, turn.

Row 2: Sc in 2nd ch from hook, hdc in eon 2 ch, dc in eon 10 sts, hdc in eon 2 ch, sc in next ch, sl st to last ch. Attach C, ch 1. Break off B.

Rows 3 & 4: Sl st in first st, sc in next st, hdc in eon 2 sts, dc in eon 10 sts, hdc in eon 2 sts, sc in next st, sl st to turning ch. Ch 1, turn.

Row 5: Sl st across first 4 sts, sc in eon 10 sts, sl st across last 4 sts. Fasten off.

With right side facing, attach A, work 1 row sl st around yellow sides.

LEGS (make 2): Ch 13 with C, sc in 2nd ch from hook, sc in next ch, hdc in each of next 2 ch, dc in eon 7 ch, hdc in last ch. Fasten off.

EYES (make 2): Ch 4 with D, join with sl st, ch 2, work 8 hdc in ring, join with sl st. Break off. Attach C, ch 1, sl st loosely around. Fasten off.

To finish, match narrow ends of legs to 3rd A row and sew to body so that wide ends extend ½″ below A rows. With D, cut four 4″ strands, and double knot two to each end of leg. Sew eyes to head. To make loop, attach B between eyes, ch 18, sl st in same sp as attached. Fasten off, weave in ends. Block.

apple approx. 8½″ x 7″

Colors: White (A), light yellow (B), yellow (C), red (D), dark green (E).

FIRST HALF: With A, ch 16.

Row 1: Sc in 2nd ch from hook, sc in next ch and in each ch across (15 sts), ch 1, turn.

Row 2: Sl st across first 5 sts, ch 1, sc in next st, dc in eon 3 sts, sc in next st, sl st across last 5 sts. With B ch 1, turn.

Row 3: Sc in eon 5 sl sts, hdc in next st, dc in eon 3 sts, hdc in next st, sc in last 5 sl sts, ch 1, turn.

Row 4: Sl st across first 5 sts, ch 1, sc in next st, hdc in next st, dc in eon 2 sts, hdc in next st, sc in next st, sl st across last 5 sts, attach C, ch 1, turn.

Row 5: 2 sc in first sl st, sc in eon 2 sts, hdc in eon 3 sts, dc in eon 4 sts, hdc in eon 3 sts, sc in eon 2 sts, 2 sc in last st, ch 1, turn.

Row 6: 2 sc in first st, sc in eon 3 sts, hdc in eon 3 sts, dc in next st, 2 dc in next st, dc in eon 2 sts, hdc in eon 3 sts, sc in eon 3 sts, 2 sc in last st, ch 1, turn.

Row 7: Sc in first st, hdc in eon 2 sts, dc in eon 15 sts, hdc in eon 2 sts, sc in last st. Fasten off.

SECOND HALF: Make the same as first half.

Join halves by sewing together with A. With right side facing, attach D to bottom, just before first B st, ch 1, work 1 row sc around edge, ending at A on bottom. Attach D to top edge, ch 1, sc, work hdc across top, dec 1 st when working over A, end sc, sl st across last 2 sts on left edge. For loop, attach A to top, ch 10, join where attached. Fasten off. Block.

LEAF: With E, ch 10, sc in 2nd ch from hook, hdc in eon 2 ch, dc in eon 3 ch, hdc in eon 2 ch, sc in last ch. Ch 1, turn.

Row 2: Sc in first st, hdc in eon 2 sts, dc in eon 3 sts, hdc in eon 2 sts, sc in last st. Fasten off. Sew to top of apple.

With chartreuse, embroider a row down the center between A and B, then between B and C. With black, make 4 or 5 French knots for seeds.

Butterfly design potholder crocheted with rug yarn.

Potholders can also be used as wall decorations to brighten up the kitchen. Shown are three designs: ladybug, frog, and apple.

Rugs

The rugs on this page, one looped, the other flat, are made in diamond-shaped sections of light and dark colors. When finished these sections can be joined in any manner of combinations. Both rugs are worked in variations of a simple increase/decrease pattern, the looped one around a cardboard strip. Because different techniques are used in making the rugs, each produces a contrasting texture. Yet another texture can be seen in the striped rug (page 63). Here heavy yarn is used double throughout in a crossed single crochet stitch and is crocheted quickly on a jumbo-sized hook. The use of doubled yarn gives body to the piece and increases its wearability. All three projects are good as experiments for combining colors.

(Left) Diamond sections in single crochet loop stitch. Join to form rug.

(Below) Diamond sections worked in half double crochet. Can be joined to form rug, or other items such as bedspread, throw, or placemat.

loop diamond rug

Materials: Aunt Lydia's Heavy Rug Yarn.
One 70-yd. skein makes 3 diamonds.
F crochet hook.
1 cardboard strip, 1″ wide, any length.

Gauge: 3 sts = 1″; 3 rows = 1″

TO MAKE ONE DIAMOND, 3½″ x 8½″: Ch 2 to begin.

Row 1: (right side) Sc in 2nd ch from hook, ch 1, turn.

Row 2: (Insert hook into first st, hold cardboard strip at back of work and against pr r, wrap yarn around strip, yo and draw through a lp, yo and draw through 2 lps on hook—loop st made)2x. Rep for next st, ch 1, turn. Remove cardboard.

Row 3: Sc in each sc across, ch 1, turn.

Row 4: 2 lp sts in first st, 1 lp st in next st and in each st across, ending 2 lp sts in last st, ch 1, turn.

Row 5: Same as row 3.

Rep rows 4 and 5 for pattern.

Work pattern rows until there are 14 lps. Work 1 row sc across, then, continuing in pattern, dec 1 lp at beg and end of each lp st row until 4 lps remain. Work 2 sc in one. Fasten off. **To dec lp st:** (insert hook into next st, wrap yarn around strip, yo and draw through a lp)2x, yo and through 3 lps on hook. Make as many diamonds as desired and join (see page 62 for suggested patterns). Edges can be squared off if desired by making triangles and adding where needed.

If you wish to make rectangular shapes instead of diamond ones, ch desired length and work as follows:

Row 1: Sc in 2nd ch from hook, and in each ch across, ch 1, turn.

Row 2: Make a lp st in first st and in each st across, ch 1, turn.

Row 3: Sc in first st and in each st across, ch 1, turn.

Rep rows 2 and 3 for pattern.

The diamond principle can be applied to a flat rug (without loops), or to a throw or bedspread made with finer yarn. (The sampler, page 60 bottom, was made with "Celtagil," Fibre Yarn Co, and an F crochet hook; 3 oz. makes 10 diamonds; gauge, 4 hdc = 1″; 6 rows = 2″.) To make one diamond, ch 3.

Row 1: Hdc in 3rd ch from hook, ch 2, turn.

Row 2: 2 hdc in st, ch 2, turn.

Row 3: 2 hdc in each st, ch 2, turn.

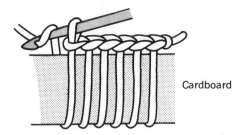

Cardboard

Working loop stitch over cardboard strip. Hold horizontally or vertically.

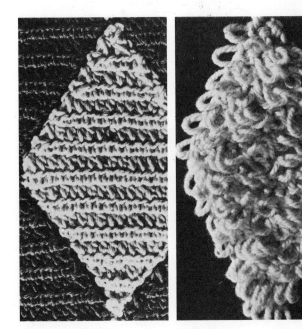

Flat-stitch diamond.   Loop-stitch diamond.

36 diamond sections

40 diamond sections

Two design arrangements for diamond sections. For squared off edges, add triangles. Triangles and diamonds can be combined or worked alone for a variety of patchwork designs.

Detail of striped rug. Note directions of crossed single crochet stitches.

Row 4: 2 hdc in first st, hdc in each of next 2 sts, 2 hdc in last st, ch 2, turn.

Continue to inc in first and last st of each row until there are 20 sts.

Next row: Yo and draw a lp through first st, keep lp on hook, yo and draw a lp through 2nd st, yo and through 5 lps on hook (1 hdc dec), hdc in each st across to last 2 sts, yo and draw a lp through next to last st, yo and draw a lp through last st, yo and through 5 lps on hook (1 hdc dec). Ch 2, turn.

Continue to dec in first and last st of each row until 1 st remains. Fasten off.

striped rug 26″ x 40″

Materials: Columbia Minerva Washable Rug Yarn, 1¾ oz. skeins.
Q crochet hook.
6 skeins tangerine (color A)
5 skeins bright yellow (color B)
4 skeins dark gold (color C)

Gauge: 3 sc = 2″; 5 rows = 4″

PATTERN STITCH: Crossed sc. Chain is an uneven number. *Note:* Use two strands as one throughout.

With 2 strands of color A, ch 41.

Row 1: Sc in 2nd ch from hook and in each ch across (40 sts). Ch 1, turn.

Row 2: Sk first st, sc in 2nd st, sc in skipped st (crossed sc made), * sk 1 st, sc in next st, sc in sk st, rep from * across, ch 1, turn.

Row 3: Sc in each st across, ch 1, turn.

Row 4: Rep row 2.

Row 5: Rep row 3 except on last yo of row drop 1 strand A, add 1 strand B.

Rep rows 2 and 3 for pattern.

Work in pattern with the following colors:

5 rows with A & B	5 rows with A & B
5 rows with B	3 rows with B
5 rows with B & C	3 rows with B & C
5 rows with C	3 rows with C
5 rows with C & A	3 rows with C & A
5 rows with A	3 rows with A

Fasten off, weave in ends. **Block.**

Striped rug, 26″ x 40″. The use of doubled yarn forms a thick, sturdy rug and allows for the blending of colors.

Soft white raffia hat with ribbon.

Hats and Ski Band

The white hat on the facing page is worked in raffia straw; its brim dips softly as here or can curve upward to frame the face. The featherweight straw makes the hat ideal for summer wear. The dominant stitch is double crochet worked in rounds; filet mesh provides the space for ribbon insertion. Single and half double crochet are combined in the ski band. Motifs are sewn onto the earflaps for a light contrasting touch. The tri-color hat is crocheted in alternating bands and strips. The stitch is raised double crochet worked in tall triangular sections that are joined when finished.

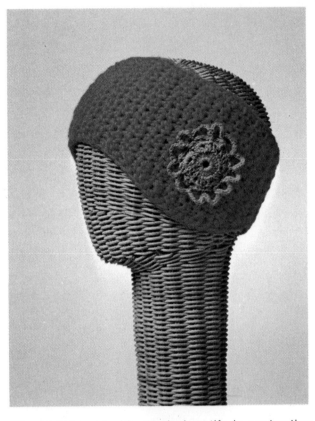

(Above) Ski band with attached motifs in contrasting color. Motif for one side is shown.

(Left) The tri-color hat is peaked here so that alternating design can be seen.

Detail of raffia hat showing ribbon inserted through a filet mesh row.

raffia hat

Materials: Raffia, three 75-yd. spools. F crochet hook. 1½ yds. of ½" ribbon.

Gauge: 4 dc = 1"; 3 dc rows = 2"

PATTERN STITCH: Dc in rounds.

Ch 5, join with sl st to form ring.

Rnd 1: Ch 3 (counts as first st), work 11 dc in ring (12 dc), join with sl st to top of ch-3.

Rnd 2: Ch 3, 1 dc in join, 2 dc in each st around (24 dc), join to top of ch-3.

Rnd 3: Ch 3, * 2 dc in next st, 1 dc in next st, rep from * around (36 dc), join to top of ch-3.

Rnd 4: Ch 3, * 2 dc in next st, 1 dc in each of next 2 sts, rep from * around (48 dc), join to top of ch-3.

Rnd 5: Ch 3, * 2 dc in next st, 1 dc in each of next 3 sts, rep from * around (60 dc), join to top of ch-3.

Rnd 6: Ch 3, * 2 dc in next st, 1 dc in each of next 4 sts, rep from * around (72 dc), join to top of ch-3.

Rnd 7: Ch 3, 1 dc in each st around (72 dc), join to top of ch-3.

Rep rnd 7 four more times.

Next rnd: (Filet mesh) Ch 4, * sk 1 st, 1 dc in next st, ch 2, rep from * around, join to top of ch-3.

BRIM:

Rnd 1: Ch 3, * 4 dc in next ch-2 sp of pr r, 3 dc in next ch-2 sp of pr r, rep from * around, join to top of ch-3.

Rnd 2: Ch 3, dc in each st around, join to top of ch-3. Turn.

Rnds 3 & 4: Same as rnd 2.

Rnd 5: (Filet mesh) Ch 4, * sk next st, dc in next st, ch 1, rep from * around, join to 3rd ch of ch-4.

Rnd 6: Ch 3, * dc in ch-1 sp, dc in next st, rep from * around, join to top of ch-3. Fasten off.

Insert ribbon through first filet mesh rnd and tie in a bow.

ski band with motif

Materials: Knitting worsted, 2 oz. I crochet hook.

Gauge: 4 sts = 1"; 10 rows = 3"

PATTERN STITCH: Sc over hdc. Chain is an uneven number.

Starting in back, ch 11.

Row 1: Sc in 2nd ch from hook, hdc in next ch, * sc in next ch, hdc in next ch, rep from * across. (10 sts) Ch 1, turn.

Row 2: Sc in first st, hdc in next st * sc in next st, hdc in next st, rep from * across. Ch 1, turn.

Rep row 2 until piece measures 2″.

FIRST EARFLAP:

Row 1: Sc, hdc in first st (inc made), sc in next st, * hdc in next st, sc in next st, rep from * across. Ch 1, turn.

Keeping in pattern, inc on same edge every row for 2 rows. Keeping in pattern, inc on same edge every *other* row for 4 rows. Work even (without inc or dec) for 5 rows. Keeping in pattern, dec one st every other row for 4 rows. Then work even until piece measures 12″. Front of ski band made.

SECOND EARFLAP: Keeping in pattern, inc 1 st every row on shaped edge for 4 rows, work even for 5 rows, dec 1 st every other row on shaped edge for 2 rows, dec 2 sts every row on shaped edge for 3 rows, work even for 2″. Fasten off. Sew back seam. If desired, adapt any motif in book and sew one on each earflap. (See photo, page 65.) Use Coats & Clark Knit-Cro-Sheen and #8 steel crochet hook.

Detail of ski band showing single and half double crochet stitches combined in a pattern.

tri-color hat

Materials: Sport yarn, 2-oz. each: black (A), red (B), green (C). G crochet hook.

Gauge: 5 dc = 1″; 6 rows = 2″

PATTERN STITCH: Raised dc. Chain is an even number.

With A, ch 20.

Row 1: Sc in 2nd ch from hook and in each ch across, ch 3, turn.

Row 2: Dc in 2nd st and in each st across, ch 1, turn.

Row 3: Sc in first st, * sc under bar of next dc (diag.), sc in next st, rep from * across. Ch 3, turn.

Rep rows 2 and 3 for pattern. Work in pattern for 2½″, change to B, work 2 rows, change to A, work 2″, change to C. Working in pattern with C, dec one st at beg and end of every 6th row. When C measures 6½″, change to B, work 2 rows, change to C. Continue to dec every 6th row until 3 sts remain. Fasten off. Make 4 more triangles, varying color positions and placements of stripes.

To finish, block triangles and sew together. Weave a doubled strand through top of hat, pull to tighten, then knot. Attach A to bottom row and work sc around. Dec 5 sts on each row, work 2 more rows with A, 3 rows with C. With B, work 3 rows even. Fasten off. Make tassel with the three colors and attach to top.

Detail of tri-color hat showing ridge design of raised double crochet.

Working under double crochet bar. Hook shows direction of stitch.

Hat and Scarf Sets

Variegated knitting worsted and the cluster stitch combine to give a highly textured look to the pink hat and scarf set on the facing page. The hat is worked in rounds; the scarf in short rows. In the red and navy set, the hat is worked widthwise like a narrow scarf and is seamed together at the finish; the scarf is crocheted lengthwise on a long chain. Both are done in a single crochet ridge stitch.

variegated hat

Materials: Knitting worsted, 4 oz. J crochet hook.

Gauge: 3 clusters = 2″; 2 rows = 2″

PATTERN STITCH: Cluster (cl) in rnds. *(Note:* Pull up a long first lp in each dc.)

Ch 5, join to form ring.

Rnd 1: Ch 3, work 8 dc in ring, join to top of ch-3.

Rnd 2: Ch 3, work 2 dc (cl) in sp between each dc, end dc in last sp (9 cls), join to top of ch-3.

Rnd 3: Ch 3, * sk 1 dc, cl in next sp, sk 2 dc, cl in next sp, rep from * around, end dc in join sp. Join to top of ch-3.

Rnd 4: Ch 3, * (sk 2 dc, cl in next sp)2x, (sk 1 dc, cl in next sp)2x, rep from *, end dc in join sp. Join to top of ch-3.

Rnds 5–8: Rep row 4, except work first half of rep as follows: 3x for rnd 5, 4x for rnd 6, 5x for rnd 7, 6x for rnd 8. (2nd half of rep is worked 2x throughout).

Rnds 9–12: Ch 3, work (sk 2 dc, cl in next sp) around, end dc in join sp. Join to top of ch-3.

Rnd 13: Ch 1, work sc in each st around. Join.

Work 4 more sc rnds, dec 3 sts evenly each rnd. Fasten off. Make pompon and sew to top of hat.

variegated scarf 10″ x 60″ (excluding fringe)

Knitting worsted, 8 oz. Same hook and gauge as hat. Pull up dc lp as above.

Ch 28 to start.

Row 1: Dc in 4th ch from hook and in each ch across, ch 3, turn.

Row 2: Sk 1 dc, dc in next sp, (sk 2 dc, 2 dc in next sp) across, ch 3, turn.

Row 3: (sk 2 dc, 2 dc in next sp) across, end dc in top of ch-3.

Rep rows 2 and 3 until piece measures 60″ or desired length. Fasten off. Add a fringe 6″ long at each end.

red and navy hat

Materials: Knitting worsted, 2 oz. each: red and navy. K crochet hook.

Gauge: 3 sc = 1″; 4 rows = 1″

PATTERN STITCH: Sc ridge st.

With navy, ch 28.

Row 1: Sc in 2nd ch and in each ch across, ch 1, turn.

Row 2: Sc in *back* lp of each st across, ch 1, turn.

Row 3: Rep row 2.

Row 4: Sc in back lp of first st, * sc in back lp of next st, rep from * 21x (shaping of hat). Ch 1, turn.

Row 5: Sc in back lp across. Attach red, ch 1, turn.

Row 6: With red rep row 2 including sts not worked on row 4.

Rows 7–9: Rep row 2, working rows 8–9 in navy.

Rep rows 4–9 as follows: 6 red rows, 4 navy, 4 red, 6 navy, 2 red, 4 navy, 4 red, 2 navy, 6 red, 4 navy, 4 red, 6 navy, 2 red, 4 navy, 6 red, 2 navy, 6 red.

Sew first and last rows tog. Weave a doubled strand through end st of each long row, draw tight and fasten. To make band, attach navy to back seam, work 1 sc rnd (53 sts), join to first st. Turn to wrong side and work sc under bar of next sc (work as in diagram on page 67) for 5 rnds. Fasten off. Make pompon and sew to hat.

red and navy scarf 72″ x 8″ (with fringe)

Same materials (4 oz. each color) and gauge as hat. With navy, make a ch 60″ long. Work rows 1 and 2 as for hat. Rep row 2 for 4 more navy rows, then work 4 red rows, 2 navy, 6 red, 4 navy, 2 red, 2 navy. Fasten off. Add a 6″ fringe to each end.

(Right) Red and navy matching hat and scarf. (Below) Matching hat and scarf crocheted with variegated yarn.

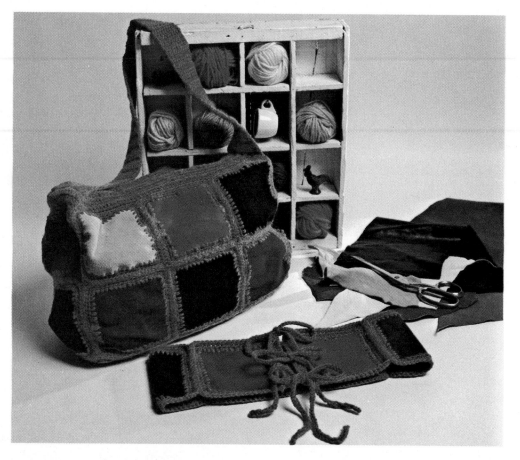

Suede purse and matching belt are made by crocheting together suede squares of different colors.

Clutch purse and belt of rattail rayon.

Shoulder bag with flower motifs.

Purses, Belts, and Shoulder Bag

The purse and matching belt on the facing page are made of plain square shapes cut out of suede (leather can also be used). The texture and pattern of the crochet stitches used to join the pieces contrast well with the smooth or shiny surfaces of the squares. A good use for scrap materials and leftover yarns. (Facing page, below left) Satiny rattail yarn provides a touch of elegance to this purse and belt worked in the very interesting single crochet weave. The purse is made in one piece. The white shoulder bag, worked in a variation of the cluster stitch, uses heavy rug yarn and a jumbo-sized hook. Small motifs are crocheted separately and sewn on for color accent.

suede handbag

Materials: Nineteen 4″ squares of suede or leather. Columbia Minerva Nantuk Sport Yarn, 2 skeins, copper or heather (for bag *and* belt). B crochet hook. Awl or leather punch. 12″ zipper.

With awl or leather punch make holes around each square ⅛″ from edge, ¼″ apart. Attach yarn to any hole and work as follows:

Rnd 1: Work sc in each hole, 3 sc in each corner hole. Join with sl st to first st. Do not turn.

Rnds 2 & 3: Sc in each st, 3 sc in each corner st. Join with sl st to first st. Do not turn.

Fasten off. Sew squares together as shown.

FLAPS: With right side facing, work 1 sc row across top 3 squares at front of bag, ch 3, turn. Dc in 2nd st, dc in each st across, ch 3, turn. Work 4 more dc rows. Fasten off. Rep for back of bag. Sew flaps to end sides and sew zipper along center of both flaps.

STRAP: Work 1 dc row across end square of one side, continue working dc rows, dec at each end until 10 dc remain. Work even on 10 dc until strap measures 34″, or desired length, inc 1 dc at each end until there are 20 dc. Fasten off. Sew to end square of other side.

suede belt

Five 4″ squares make a 26″ belt. Work squares as for bag and sew tog. Make six 12″ lengths of double ch. Sew to belt for tying.

Detail of suede squares. Note edgings of single crochet rows and the manner of joining.

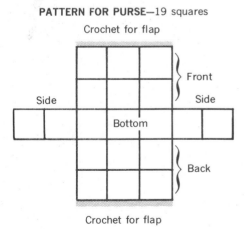

PATTERN FOR PURSE—19 squares

Crochet for flap

Side · Front · Side · Bottom · Back

Crochet for flap

clutch purse 10″ x 15½″

Materials: Fibre Yarn Co., rattail rayon #2. F crochet hook. Size 4 snap. 12″ length of hat wire.

110 yds. color A   55 yds. color B   12 yds. color C

Gauge: 7 sc = 2″; 4 rows = 1″

PATTERN STITCH: Single crochet weave. Chain is an even number.

With A, ch 36.

Row 1: Working over hat wire, sc in 2nd ch from hook and in each ch across (35 sts). Ch 1, turn.

Row 2: Attach B (tie to A strand). Keeping B in back of work, sc in first st with A, * bring B to front of work, sc in next st with A, bring B to back of work sc just made. Keeping B in back, sc in next st with A (thus weaving B in front and back of A), rep from * across. Ch 1, turn.

Row 3: Bring B around edge to back of work, sc in first st with A, * bring B to front, sc in next st with A, bring B to back across sc just made, sc in next st with A, rep from * across. Ch 1, turn.

Rep row 3 for pattern until piece measures 10″. Break off A. With B, ch 1, turn. Sc in next st and in each st across. Ch 1, turn. Work sc rows for 2″. Work last ch 1 with C.

Next row: Keeping B in back, sc in first st with C, * bring B to front, sc in next st with C, bring B to back across sc just made. Keeping B in back, sc in next st with C, rep from * across, ch 1, turn.

Rep row 3 for 1″ except, for A read C. Fasten off.

To finish, weave in ends, fold wire ends and sew over them to keep in place. Fold bottom half of piece to the point where color B begins. Sew side seams. Fold top over for flap, sew snap under flap and in the center.

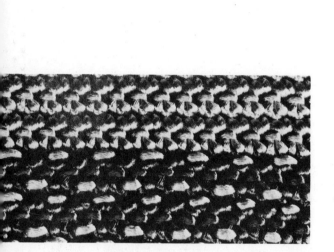

Detail of clutch purse showing pattern of single crochet weave.

belt

Materials: Fibre Yarn Co., rattail rayon #2. F crochet hook. 2″ buckle.

50 yds. color A   10 yds. color B   5 yds. color C

For a belt 2″ x 30″, ch 8 with color A, work rows 1 to 3 as for purse, rep row 3 for pattern until piece measures 28″. Work 2″ of sc with B. Work 1″ in sc weave with B and C. To finish, sew buckle to belt.

white shoulder bag 12″ x 14″

Materials: Aunt Lydia's Heavy Rug Yarn, three 70-yd. skeins. #15 wooden crochet hook.

Gauge: 1 cluster = 1″

PATTERN STITCH: Variation of cluster (cl). Multiple of 2 + 5 ch.

Ch 29 for one side of bag.

Row 1: (right side) Draw up lp in 2nd ch from hook and in each of next 3 ch (5 lps on hook), yo and pull through 5 lps on hook (cluster made), ch 1 (eye of cl), * insert hook into eye and pull through lp, insert hook into last ch of previous cl and pull through lp, pull up a lp in each of next 2 ch (5 lps on hook), yo and pull through 5 lps on hook, ch 1, rep from * across. Ch 1, turn.

Row 2: Sc in first ch (eye) and in each st and ch across. Ch 3, turn.

Row 3: Pull up 1 lp each in 2nd and 3rd ch of ch-3, pull up lp in each of first 2 sts (5 lps on hook), yo and pull through 5 lps on hook, ch 1, * pull up lp in eye, pull up lp in last st of previous cl, pull up lp in each of next 2 sts, yo and pull through 5 lps on hook, ch 1, rep from * across. Ch 1, turn.

Rep rows 2 and 3 for 13 more rows. Fasten off. Make other side of bag exactly the same.

GUSSET AND HANDLE: Ch 7, work in pattern until piece measures 40″. Fasten off. Sew to both sides of bag.

Detail of shoulder bag shows clustering of stitches.

FLOWER MOTIF: With leftover knitting worsted, ch 5, join with sl st to form ring. In center of ring work (1 sc, ch 4, 1 tr, ch 4) 6x. Sl st to first sc. Fasten off. Make as many as you wish and sew onto bag.

To spark your imagination. A jewelry assortment of earrings, choker, and pendant. Vary designs as you please.

jewelry

By crocheting silver or gold lamé thread over plastic curtain rings, then sewing them together, you can fashion a choker, earrings, or pendant. To vary, try out different combinations. Belts can also be made in this manner and can be fastened with a bead closing.

Materials: 2-ply silver or gold lamé thread, 75-yd. spool. #7 steel crochet hook. Utility plastic rings: ⅝″ (choker, earrings); ⅝″, ⅞″, 1⅛″ (pendant).

CHOKER: Knot thread around ring, ch 1, work 31 sc in ring, join with sl st. For next round, * ch 4, sk 2 sts, sc in next st, rep from * around. Join with sl st. Fasten off. Make 11 rings or amount to fit around neck. Place rings side by side and sew meeting loops together. For ties, attach thread to a lp of each end ring, ch 50, sc in 2nd ch from hook and in each ch to end. To add beads, sew one to the center of each ring and between each ring.

EARRINGS: Make 4 rings as above and sew 2 together for each earring. Attach beads and ear fastenings.

PENDANT: Work 1 hdc rnd in each ring until filled. Sew rings in design shown or in your own design. To make pendant chain, attach thread to top ring on one side, ch 1. Work 3 sc, ch 1, turn. Continue 3 sc rows until chain measures 13″ or desired length. Fasten off. Sew to top ring on other side. Ring design can also be sewn to belts or collars.

Lace trim. A succession of floral motifs joined while being made.

lace trim

FIRST MOTIF: Coats & Clark Knit-Cro-Sheen in various colors or the same color. #8 steel hook. Ch 5, join with sl st to form ring.

Rnd 1: In ring work (sc, ch 4, tr, ch 4)6x, join to first sc. Fasten off.

Rnd 2: Attach yarn to any tr, sc in same place, * ch 6, sc in 4th ch from hook, ch 2 (picot = pc made), sc in next tr, rep from *, end ch 6, sc in 4th ch from hook, ch 2, join to first sc.

Rnd 3: In join work (sc, ch 3, sc), * ch 9, sk pc, (sc, ch 3, sc) in next sc, rep from *, end ch 9, sk pc, join to first sc. Fasten off.

Rep rnds 1 & 2 for as many motifs as you wish. Attach motifs as follows: (rnd 3 for 2nd motif) in join work (sc, ch 3, sc), ch 4. Sc in lp of first motif. (2nd motif) ch 4, sk pc, (sc, ch 3, sc) in next sc, ch 4. Sc in next lp on first motif. (2nd motif) ch 4, sk pc, (sc, ch 3, sc) in next sc, continue from row 3 rep. Fasten off. Attach next motif; 2nd motif will now become first motif and so on.

crocheting with beads

It is possible to add an occasional bead or a bead design to any of the motifs or patterns that have been given. The process, a simple one, is as follows: String the required number of beads onto the thread that will be used. Push beads down out of the way, make starting chain and crochet as usual. Whenever a bead is to be used, push it up to the hook, hold in front of work and make the next stitch around it. Then continue as usual.

window hanging

For a creative approach to the use of motifs try a geometric design. The window hanging is made with pearl cotton and is based on the repetition of seven motifs. The motifs are made separately, then joined and attached to a crocheted hoop.

Materials: Coats & Clark Pearl Cotton, seven 50-yd. balls. #9 steel crochet hook. 10″ wooden ring (or inner ring of embroidery hoop).

PATTERN STITCH: Motif with clusters and picots.

TO MAKE ONE MOTIF, 3¼″: Ch 6, join with sl st to form ring.

Rnd 1: Ch 3 (counts as first st), work 11 dc in ring, join with sl st to top of ch-3.

Rnd 2: Ch 4 (counts as 1 dc and 1 ch), * dc in next st, ch 1, rep from * around, join to 3rd ch of ch-4 (12 dc with ch 1 between).

Rnd 3: Ch 3, (yo, insert hook in join, pull up a lp)4x (9 lps), yo and through 8 lps on hook, yo and through 2 lps on hook (4 dc cl made), ch 3, * (yo, insert hook into next st, pull up a lp)5x (11 lps), yo and through 10 lps on hook, yo and through 2 lps on hook (cl), ch 3, rep from * around. Join to first cl.

Rnd 4: Ch 3, 4 dc in ch-3 sp of pr r, * dc in next cl, 4 dc in next ch-3 sp, rep from * around (60 dc). Join to top of ch-3.

Rnd 5: * Sc between next 2 sts (over cl), ch 6, sk 5 sts, rep from * around. Join to first st.

Rnd 6: * In ch-6 sp work (4 sc, ch 4, sc in 4th ch from hook [picot], 4 sc), rep from * around. Join to first st.

Fasten off. Rep for 6 more motifs. Do a row of sc around ring. Join round and make an 18″ chain for hanging.

Block each motif; place 6 in a circle with the 7th in center. Sew together by joining two picots of each motif. Sew joined motifs to ring.

(Above) Window hanging of seven motifs. Considered a good luck charm in Sweden. Joined motifs are attached to crochet-covered wooden hoop. (Below) Detail of one motif shows joining of picots.

"Owl," wall hanging, 9½" x 16", worked in single crochet throughout.

wall hanging 9½" x 16"

Inspired by an African wooden mask depicting an owl, this wall hanging uses sport and slub yarns and is in single crochet throughout. The use of this stitch provides a closely worked, neutral background upon which a three-color design can be effectively seen. The wall hanging is small and its purpose is to introduce you to the possibilities of creative design in crochet.

Materials: Sport yarn, 2-oz. skeins, 1 skein each: black, rust. Botany Ping Pong (slub yarn), 40-gr. skeins, 2 skeins white #802. C crochet hook. Bobbins.

Gauge: 5 sts = 1"

Note: If yarn has to be carried across more than 3 sts, attach new bobbin. Always carry yarn loosely across wrong side of work.

Ch 46 with black. (The piece is crocheted from top to bottom.)

Row 1: Sc in 2nd ch from hook and in each ch across. Attach rust and ch 1. Turn.

Row 2: With rust sc in first st working last yo and pulling through with black (color changes are made by pulling new color through with last yo). With black, sc in each of next 2 sts, attach white, sc in each of next 2 sts, carrying black loosely across back of work sc in each of next 2 sts with black, carrying white across back sc in each of next 2 sts with white. Attach black, sc in each of next 25 sts, attach white, sc in each of next 2 sts, attach black, sc in each of next 2 sts, carrying white across back sc in each of next 2 sts with white, carrying black across back sc in each of next 2 sts with black, attach rust, sc in each of next 2 sts, ch 1 with black, turn.

Rows 3–78: Continue working sc, following color changes on graph.

TO MAKE EYES: Directions below are for one eye; rep for other. With white ch 6, join with sl st to form ring.

Rnd 1: Ch 1, work 10 sc in ring. Attach black, join with sl st.

Rnd 2: With black ch 1, 2 sc in first st, * sc in next st, 2 sc in next st, rep from * around, join to first st with rust.

Rnd 3: With rust ch 1, sc in first st, 2 sc in next st, * sc in each of next 2 sts, 2 sc in next st, rep from * around. Join to first st with black.

Rnd 4: With black ch 1, * 2 sc in next st, sc in each of next 3 sts, join to first st with white.

Rnd 5: With white, sl st in each st around. Fasten off.

To finish, block, sew eyes in place. Make a 4-strand, 6" fringe as indicated on graph.

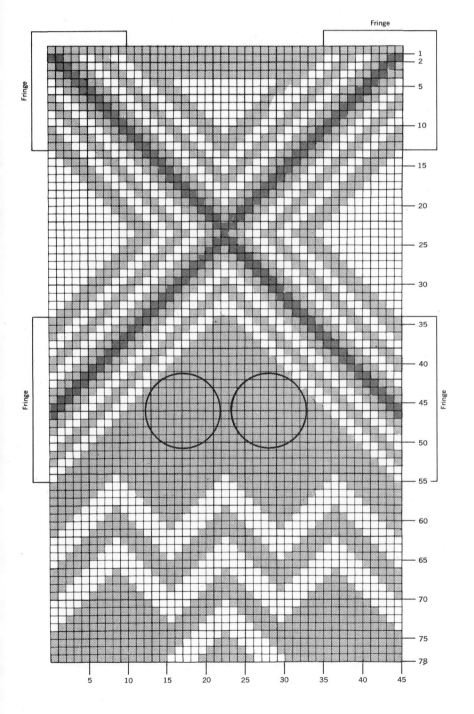

Detail of wall hanging showing color changes worked in single crochet.

Hairpin Lace Crochet

With a hairpin loom you can crochet lace strips to use as decorative edging, to insert between areas of solid crochet, or to join for items such as placemats, stoles, tablecloths, or afghans. Looms come in several shapes and adjust to various widths.

Hairpin lace placemat of 10/2 linen. 17½" x 12".

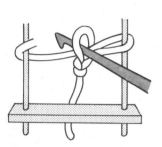

Starting of lace strip. One chain stitch made.

3 STEPS IN MAKING LACE STRIP

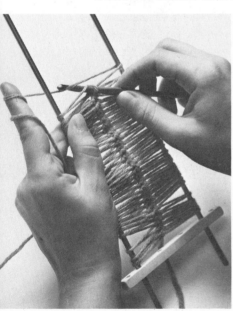

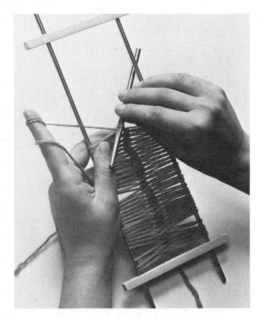

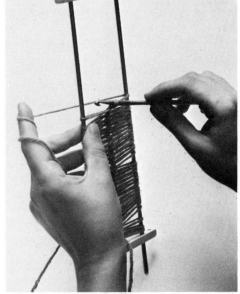

1. Single crochet being made.

2. Turn hook end down, other end behind prong. Turn loom right to left toward you.

3. Bring hook into crochet position. Work an sc. Note that loops are pushed down while working.

TO MAKE A LACE STRIP:

1. Begin with a slip knot as usual. Hold loom in left hand; hold hook between prongs. Wrap yarn front to back around right-hand prong, yo, and pull through 1 ch (diag., facing page).

2. Turn hook as shown (center photo). Turn loom from right to left toward you (yarn will automatically wind around right-hand prong). Bring hook into crochet position, work 1 sc under top left lp.

Rep step 2 throughout. Push lps down as you work. When loom becomes crowded, remove bottom bar and slip off all but 4 lps. Replace bar. If a lot of lps are being made, keep count by marking every 25th one on each side. For easier joining, twist lps when inserting hook.

lace placemat 17½" x 12"

Materials: Frederick Fawcett's 10/2 linen, 1 oz. #2 steel crochet hook. Hairpin loom set at 1½" width.

Gauge: 5 lps = 1"

Working 2 sc into each left-hand lp make 6 strips, each one with 75 lps on each side. Join by placing strips side by side. Attach yarn at top or bottom, ch 1, insert hook *back* to *front* (this twists st) through first 3 lps on right-hand strip, sc, ch 3, insert hook *front* to *back* through first 3 lps on left-hand strip, sc, * ch 3, insert *back* to *front* through next 3 lps on right, sc, ch 3, insert *front* to *back* through next 3 lps on left, sc, rep * to end. Fasten off. Attach next strip.

To finish short edge, attach yarn to one side, and, keeping work flat, do 1 row sc along edge, turn, sl st in each st across. Fasten off and do other edge. Block.

Other ways to join lace strips are described below and are shown to the right. You can also join with a favorite pattern stitch.

A. (top) Attach yarn, work sc in each lp of each strip, ch 1, turn, sc in sc. Fasten off. Join strips by weaving through sc rows.

B. (center) Attach yarn, pick up 3 lps of right strip, sc, (pick up next lp of left strip and sc)3x, * pick up 6 lps of right strip, sc, (pick up next lp of left strip and sc)6x, rep from *, end (pick up lp of left strip and sc)3x, pick up 3 lps of right strip, and sc.

C. (bottom) With hook pick up first 3 lps of left strip, then first 3 lps of right strip, pull right strip lps through left strip lps on hook. Pick up next 3 lps of left strip and pull through right strip lps on hook. Continue in this fashion. At end thread a needle with matching yarn and sew remaining 3 lps flat for a smooth edge.

METHODS OF JOINING STRIPS

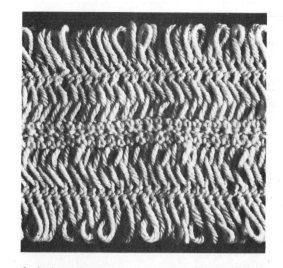

A. Strips joined with single crochet for a flat look.

B. Contrasting edges—one gathered, the other straight.

C. Braided effect worked by pulling loops through in groups.

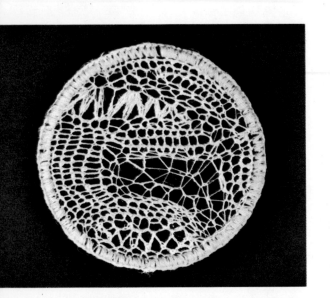

Crocheted wall piece, 8″ diameter, worked in linen. 1967. By Robert H. Goodman. Courtesy of The American Crafts Council.

Multiple of Stitches

For definition and purpose, see page 26. Pattern stitches and projects are listed in the order they appear in the book.

Shell st	6+4	Yellow Stole	Uneven no.
Filet mesh	Uneven no.	Placemat Pattern # 1	13+4
Open shell	6+4	Placemat Pattern #2	7+2
Cluster st	3+1	Placemat Pattern #4	20+10
Puff st	4+3	Casement	22+10
Popcorn st	4+3	Baby's Blanket	6+1
Crossed double crochet	Even no.	Striped Rug	Even no.
Solomon's knot	5+1	Clutch Purse	Uneven no.
		White Shoulder Bag	2+4
Lanyard Tote Bag	3+1	Ski Band	Uneven no.
Pink Stole	4+1	Tri-color Hat	Even no.
Mohair Shawl	Uneven no.	Variegated Scarf	Even no.

For Further Reading

Blackwell, Liz, *A Treasury of Crochet Patterns*, Charles Scribner's Sons, New York, N.Y. 1971

Maddox, Marguerite, *The Complete Book of Knitting & Crochet*, Pocket Books, New York, N.Y. Revised edition 1971

Suppliers

YARNS, Wholesale
(Write for information regarding nearest retail outlet)

Botany Yarns
Bernhard Ulmann Co.
30–20 Thomson Ave.
New York, N.Y. 11101

Coats & Clark, Inc.
72 Cummings Point Rd.
Stanford, CONN. 06902

Columbia Minerva Corp.
295 5th Ave.
New York, N.Y. 10016

Paternayan Bros. Inc.
312 E. 95th St.
New York, N.Y. 10028

William Unger & Co., Inc.
230 5th Ave.
New York, N.Y. 10001

YARNS & EQUIPMENT, Mail Order

Textile Crafts
856 N. Genesee Ave.
PO Box 3216
Los Angeles, CAL. 90028

Warp, Wool & Potpourri
514 N. Lake Ave.
Pasadena, CAL. 91101

The Yarn Depot, Inc.
545 Sutter St.
San Francisco, CAL. 94102

Macrame & Weaving Supply Co.
63 East Adams St.
Chicago, ILL. 60603

Craft Kaleidoscope
6412 Ferguson Ave.
Indianapolis, IND. 46220

Earth Guild, Inc.
149 Putnam Ave.
Cambridge, MASS. 02319

Fredrick J. Fawcett, Inc.
129 South St.
Boston, MASS. 02111

Lily Mills Co.
PO Box 88
Shelby, N.C. 28150

Coulter Studios
118 East 59th St.
New York, N.Y. 10022

Yellow Springs Strings
PO Box 107
68 Goes Station
Yellow Springs, OHIO 45387

Black Sheep Weaving & Craft Supply
318 SW 2nd St.
Corvallis, ORE. 97330

Craft Yarns of Rhode Island, Inc.
Main St.
Harrisville, R.I. 02830

Kessenich Looms & Yarn Shop
7463 Harwood Ave.
Wauwatosa, WIS. 53213